THE GOOD NEWS

Illh

Dear Z—,

I hope you know
God through this and
you continue to grow in
your love for Jesus.

Love,
Andrew

All rights reserved.

No part of this publication may be reproduced or transmitted in any form or by any means, electronic or mechanical, including photocopy, recording, or any information storage and retrieval system, without permission in writing from the author.

The author will permit up to 250 words of prose to be extracted for non-commercial purposes, or for review, subject to full acknowledgement being given to the author, title, publisher, and date of publication.

Any names and stories used in this book are done so with permission from those involved. Some names have been changed to protect the identity of those involved.

When Scripture is quoted the version is indicated by the following abbreviations:
AMP: The Amplified Bible
ESV: English Standard Version
NIV: New International Version

The right of Andrew Stansbury to be identified as authors of this work has been asserted by him in accordance with the Copyright, Designs and Patent Act 1988.

For my wife, Rebekah.

Thank you for your encouragement, faith, wisdom, kindness and perseverance. We've got there. Here is to the unknown journey, travelled together.

Thanks also to Caitlin for her amazing illustrations and patience when I wasn't making sense.

To Nat and Hannah, Tim, and Chris and Helena, for their comments, edits and feedback.

To Paul for the time he has given to thoroughly editing this book; always giving me wise feedback, delivered in a kind and clear way.

And to Jonah for his tireless work on the layout, feel and appearance of the book as a whole. His attention to detail, creative and innovative ideas and commitment to faithfully represent the content of this book, has bettered this book far more than many will realise.

CONTENTS

Map i
A pictorial representation of the journey of this book.

Foreword iii

Introduction 1

1. The Good News That Keeps Getting Better 6
   The Gospel is not just what Jesus has done for us—it is the news of Jesus Christ Himself. He is the Gospel.

2. Seekers, Finders, Minders, Keepers 24
   Discovering and fulfilling our calling is not our responsibility—it is God's. How do we re-understand calling in light of this?

3. Leaning On Nothing Until It Holds You Up 50
   How do we agree with something God says to us when we cannot yet see that with which He is asking us to agree?

4. Turning Sin Outside In 74
   Sin isn't about doing the wrong thing; it's about believing in anything, at any moment, other than Jesus.

5. Fire Isn't The Absence Of Water 104
   Instead of defining purity by what it isn't, how would we define purity by what it is?

6. Permission Or Blessing? 124
   Do we live asking God what He permits for us, or what He blesses?

7. Resetting Default Settings 144
   If, thanks to Jesus, we have become new creations, then what default mindsets can we now adopt?

8. Humble Pie 164
    Godly humility isn't about thinking lowly of yourself...

9. It's Always Time For Your Dancing Shoes 188
    What if sung worship could be what our hearts wanted to do all of the time?

10. The Dying Fish 214
    How do we hold Jesus' victory in tension with the promised turbulence of the end times?

11. Is It Hard? 240
    I was asked once whether I found being a Christian hard—this is my response.

12. The Mirror 260
    God is trying to get our attention. Will we dare to actually listen?

Epilogue 279

FOREWORD
by Rebekah Stansbury

What does it mean to truly follow Jesus?

It is a question at the very centre of what it means to be a Christian, an invitation that begins every journey into the Christian faith and continues to walk us through till the very end. We may have asked it of ourselves, or had it asked of us and, whether we wrestle with it in intimate combat, or scurry about trying to bury it in the sand of everyday activity, the fact remains that Jesus' invitation to follow Him is still there, knocking at the door.

Over the past few years, I have seen Andrew hear and respond to Jesus' knock many times, in many different ways. He has been, and continues to be, shaped by truths God has revealed to him about what following Jesus looks like, and he will not settle for anything less; it's one of the things that inspires me most about him.

But Andrew also won't settle for anything less for those around him. On countless occasions, he has been led to fight for, encourage, and teach others how to discover what this revolutionary way of life looks like for them, and I have seen it bring about many incredible transformations.

This is where The Good News That Keeps Getting Better comes from. It is an inspired unpacking of Jesus' call to follow Him, shared in a powerful and accessible way. But the beauty and uniqueness of this book is that it does not aim to give us the answers; its aim is to lead us to Jesus, for it's in Him that all answers are found.

Yes, there are many different aspects to following Jesus (if it were straightforward, we wouldn't all still be caught up trying to work out how to do it!), and Andrew unpacks many of these in incredibly helpful ways. Andrew has caught hold of something truly alive in the *The*

Good News That Keeps Getting Better; underpinning every complicated aspect of the Christian faith is the simple call to follow the person of Jesus Himself.

Do you want to step more fully into following Jesus?

Are you willing to say *"Yes!"* to all that Jesus has for you and settle for nothing less?

(For there is always more, and, as I have discovered, it keeps getting better).

Well then, let the adventure begin![1]

---

1. P.S As for Andrew? Trust him. You're in safe hands.

INTRODUCTION

Complex Simplicity

Following Jesus leads us to realise over and over again the simple fact that there is nothing of true value outside of Him.

Yet as we recognise that one simple truth, we also come to see that the person of Jesus is unparalleled in His complexities.

Apart from Him nothing has true value, and yet, as *Colossians 1.17* tells us, He is in everything, holding it all together.

This complex simplicity seems to grow ever larger the longer we walk with Him.

The simplicity of the call to follow Him, and the complexities and wonders of who He is and what He does.

Over the past five or so years, this has been my experience. Every revelation and encounter I have had with God has left me feeling refocused, and my faith simplified.

Refocused to that simple truth that there is nothing to hold onto other than Jesus.

Any other thing I try to cling onto will fade.

From my own life, and in talking with others, I have seen how easy it is to spend a lot of energy trying to cling onto our own ability to comprehend the person of Jesus.

We study His life hard, trying to understand all that He did and how we can replicate His works, assembling phrases and theories to explain what God does, and what He doesn't; who He is, and who He isn't.

But God does not fit within our theories of Him.

Our understanding of Him is expanding and growing, yet it is not complete, or total.

Our knowledge of God is always growing not because He changes, but because our human minds cannot yet fully grasp the wonder of who He is.

Fortunately for us, Jesus didn't model a faith dependent on understanding every aspect of the Father.

Jesus' faith was built on His love for the Father, and because of His love for the Father, Jesus followed and obeyed Him.

Everything Jesus did, He did by following the Father. [1]

In the same way, Jesus didn't call His disciples to understand Him.

He called them to follow Him. [2]

Those are two very distinct things.

Following Jesus is an incredibly simple task.

Simple in the sense that it is a single command. There are no hidden clauses or loopholes. It is just the one simple phrase;

"Follow me."

Throughout our lives we will find ourselves in many different situations, with many different choices before us. They are all part of the complexity of life.

---

1. *John 5.19.*
2. *Matthew 4.18-22.*

Yet at every twist and turn, we are faced with the same invitation from Jesus;

"Follow me."

Through obeying that single command, we find ourselves living a life of discovery. God will give us wisdom and understanding about Him and the world He made. He will show us mysteries and wonders far beyond our comprehension.

Yet ultimately, no matter what understandings God grants us, we must hold fast to the simple invitation from Christ to follow Him.

No matter where He goes, or what He does.

The real, breathing, walking, talking, resurrected person of Jesus.

"Follow me."

This book is a collection of re-focuses that Jesus has worked in my life. Each chapter speaks of an area of my faith where Jesus narrowed my vision and attention to just Him, and how He invited me to follow Him in the day-to-day.

Of course at times my mind wanders beyond Him and my eyes try to look outside of Him, but I know His intention is to continually bring me back to the simplicity of leaning solely on Him.

Being refocused by Jesus sometimes requires understanding to be abandoned, and sometimes furthered.

Being refocused by Him may turn us upside down, or it may just nudge us gently to the right or to the left.

My prayer for you as you read this book is that Jesus will lay hold of you and unclutter your heart and mind, so that your confidence is rooted in nothing but the living Jesus.

I do not want you to try and learn the lessons I have learnt.

My hope is that you will each be taught the specific lessons Jesus wants to teach you through the examples of what He has taught me.

They might be similar.

They might not.

I pray that each of you will find yourselves with a simple and deep desire to follow Jesus no matter where He leads, with complete assurance that His wisdom, His grace and His power will prove to be more than sufficient for you.

If we each gave ourselves to the single task of following Jesus, I wonder what complexities He might show us and where He might lead us?

The complex simplicity of following Jesus Christ:

> *The secret [of the sweet, satisfying companionship] of the Lord have they who fear (revere and worship) Him, and He will show them His covenant and reveal to them its [deep, inner] meaning.*
> PSALM 25.14 AMP

Lord, let it begin.

1. The Good News That Keeps Getting Better

I'm Here

A very good friend of mine, Emily, asked me to sit down with her and her friend Anthony, to talk through some frustrations that he was having with faith.

I love being a part of that kind of conversation, so said yes.

With Anthony opposite me and Emily next to me, Anthony began to share what was on his mind.

Over the course of a year or so, Anthony had become progressively disillusioned with the level of passion he saw in the Christians around him, especially during sung worship. In Anthony's mind, he had begun to wonder why people weren't more fiery and emotional in their love of Jesus.

How could we stand and sing before God without our hearts and emotions being profoundly moved by how kind, glorious and lovely He is?

It's a good question.

As Anthony went on, it became evident that he was in fact frustrated with his own worship and faith. Anthony felt like his faith didn't have a God who was near, or a God who was very talkative.

He didn't feel as though he had truly met the God that he was doing his best to live for.

Of course, he knew he was *meant* to say that he *"always meets with God through Scripture"*, and that *"it isn't about an emotional encounter with God"*, but nonetheless, his heart was deeply troubled by this lack of a tangible and emotional closeness with God.

From what I could gather, Anthony couldn't understand why, if God was truly active and alive, he couldn't have an encounter with God where God spoke to him and in which he could sense God's presence.

There was an incredibly deep longing in Anthony as he spoke and I didn't really know what to do. I was silenced by his honesty and his openness. It was very clear just how significant this moment was for him.

Once he'd finished talking we decided to pray, and we prayed one simple thing, largely because we didn't know what else to do.

We prayed;

"God, please would you meet with Anthony now."

Almost as soon as we had prayed, Anthony burst into tears. Emily and I didn't say anything; we just waited as he cried.

After a while, I asked Anthony what had just happened.

He told us that the moment after we had prayed that little prayer, he had heard God say to him;

"Anthony, I'm here."

Then God just kept repeating that phrase;

"I'm here."

"I'm here."

"I'm here."

Anthony then felt God say;

"What do you want to talk about?"

At this point, Anthony told Emily and me that he suddenly realised he didn't have any questions to ask God. What Anthony had been longing for was to have a tangible meeting with God so that he knew that if he ever *did* have any questions to ask, there was a listening, talkative God close by to answer them.

All of Anthony's frustrations and angst originated from one simple cry that had been burning within him to ask God;

"Are you really there?"

The Good News

The word 'Gospel' simply means 'Good News'.

To state the obvious, the Christian Gospel is Good News because it is news of something good—the person of Jesus Christ.

For some of us, when we think of telling others the Good News, we think solely about communicating what Jesus has done for humankind; that He died on our behalf to pay for our sins so that we can have access to God and enjoy that relationship for all eternity.

But the Gospel is the Good News of Jesus Christ, not just the Good News of what Jesus Christ has done.

Of course, the person of Jesus Christ includes all He has done. I am not for a moment suggesting that what Jesus has done for humankind is anything less than perfectly loving and wholly marvellous.

However, behind every deed and work is a person, and so behind all the deeds and works of Jesus, is Jesus.

For Jesus Christ *is* the Gospel.[1]

---

1. *(See bottom of next page for reference)*

The very man Himself.

What is more, thanks to the resurrection of Jesus, the Good News is not just a person who walked on earth years ago; the Good News is a person who is with us presently, in His fullness, by His Spirit.

Not only is Jesus the Good News, but the Good News is alive.

Anthony knew the Good News of what Jesus Christ had done; he knew it really well! Yet he was left with a longing for more.

As indeed, I believe all of us should be.

All that Jesus has done for us points to His ultimate invitation to be in daily, moment-by-moment communion and friendship with the very person of Jesus Himself.

Everything He did was to make a way for us to know Him; a way to be filled with the Holy Spirit, to walk with the living Jesus, and to know God the Father.

Again, please do not think I am suggesting in any way that we play down the life, death and resurrection of Jesus Christ. The sacrifice of Jesus is unimaginably awesome.

---

1. Paul refers to this in *Romans 1.1-3* where he writes:

   Paul, a servant of Christ Jesus, called to be an apostle, set apart for the gospel of God...
   concerning his Son.
   ROMANS 1.1&3 ESV

The Gospel of God, according to Paul, is about God's Son, Jesus. Paul goes on to mention some of the things Jesus did for us, but it is important to note that he starts with the person.

It is not a question of whether we have over-emphasised the works of Jesus.

That would be impossible.

However, it may be a question of whether we are each truly seeking to know the person of Jesus, as well as knowing what He has done for us.

As marvellous as the cross, resurrection and ascension of Jesus are, which is wholly marvellous, Jesus Christ Himself is more marvellous still.

His glory far surpasses the glory of any thing He has done.

The activities of God are demonstrations of His glory, but they are not the source of His glory.

God Himself is the source of His glory.

A person's benevolent acts do not totally contain or fully express who they are. Their acts of generosity flow from, and demonstrate only a part of, who they are.

And so it is with Jesus.

Anthony knew the Good News of what Jesus Christ had done, but his longing was for the person behind the works. He wanted to truly know Jesus, to talk with Him and to have Jesus as His guide.

At the beginning of this book, perhaps each of us could ask ourselves an honest question;

Have we settled for just knowing the facts of what Jesus Christ has done, or are we allowing ourselves to really search out and explore the actual person of Jesus?

The Way

> *Jesus said to him, "I am the way, and the truth, and the life. No one comes to the Father except through me."*
> JOHN 14.6 ESV

Jesus tells His disciples that He Himself is the Way.

He doesn't say that He models the Way, or that He can show them the Way.

No, He says that He *is* the Way.

So if you want to know the Way, know the person, because the person is the Way.

In the next chapter of John's Gospel, Jesus teaches His disciples to remain in Him.[2]

Jesus first tells His disciples that He Himself is the Way, and then He tells them to remain in Him.

Well that makes sense, doesn't it? If Jesus Himself is the Way, then we need to remain in Him to keep to the Way.

If we lose sight of Him, if we depart from Him, then we're lost again, even if we're trying our best to 'do the right thing' and to 'go the right way'!

Fortunately, Jesus expands on what it means to remain in Him in *John 15*:

> *As the Father has loved me, so have I loved you. Abide in my love.*
> JOHN 15.9 ESV

---

2. *John 15.4.*

Jesus tells His disciples that the way to remain in Him is to remain in His love, just as He remained in the love of His Father.

It sounds so simple, doesn't it? Just don't leave the love of God.

God is unswerving in His passion, love and commitment to you and me—His love will never leave us—but we must make choices every day, either to remain within His perfectly consistent love, or to step away from it.[3]

If we choose to remain in God's love, we will know the Way, we will love the Way, and we will proclaim the Way.

So what does it look like for us to remain wholly in the love of God?

It's a question we must each ask ourselves because, all being unique, there is no one, single answer. Whilst we can be inspired by how those around us remain in God's love, we must learn how *we* remain in His love. There will be commonalities with others, but if we tried imitating another entirely, it would never quite feel comfortable or true.

It would be a bit like wearing a jacket that has been tailor made for someone else of a similar size. The jacket is still wearable, but it doesn't feel fully comfortable, or fit us entirely well.

Let us explore for ourselves how to remain in the vast love of God.

As we set out to discover how we each remain in His love, I would like us to note two things.

Firstly, the love of God is something to experience in our hearts as well

---

[3]. If we do ever choose to step away from God's everlasting love, we must remember that His grace enables us to re-enter it without punishment. We need only heartfelt repentance. Read the story of the prodigal son in *Luke 15* to see this in action.

as to know in our minds.[4]

Just as the glory of God leads Him to do glorious things, so the love of God leads Him to do loving things.

Everything He does reflects who He is.

Throughout Scripture we see God constantly demonstrating His love for us. The sacrifice of Jesus was the greatest demonstration of God's love, but God has not stopped demonstrating His love since the cross, because God has not stopped *being* love since the cross.

Experiences of the love of God are to be expected and longed for because God is love. However, we must equally remember that any given experience of God does not contain the fullness of God Himself, as no deed can fully contain a person's character.

We must be open to experiencing the love of God, but we must not think that an absence of an experience equates to God not being loving.

Secondly, we must not set limits on how God demonstrates His love for us, to us.

---

4. *Ephesians 3.19* tells us that the love of Christ surpasses knowledge. If we do not allow God to go beyond our minds to our hearts, we will never experience the love of Christ beyond knowledge. God does not want us to abandon the mind, or ignore the heart; otherwise He wouldn't have put His new covenant in and on them:

> *For this is the covenant that I will make with the house of Israel*
> *after those days, declares the Lord:*
> *I will put my laws into their minds,*
> *and write them on their hearts,*
> *and I will be their God,*
> *and they shall be my people.*
> HEBREWS 8.10 ESV

Some people have amazing visions of the heavenly realms; some hear God speaking through pictures, words or dreams; while others find Scripture coming alive and speaking to them as God reveals its meaning. Still more find that God speaks when they are cycling, or fishing, or dancing, or simply in the quietness of their own thoughts.[5]

God is able to use anything to communicate His love to us. Even in our lowest moments He is there speaking to us, not causing the strife or pain, but communicating His affection for us in the midst of it.

We do not have to have an intensely emotional moment to experience God's affection.

Can an intensely emotional moment be a legitimate response to an experience of the Father's vast affection? Of course it can. But it is not the only way that God communicates His affection for us, to us.

Any moment in which God demonstrates His love for us is as valid as any other. We value it when God demonstrates His love not because of the demonstration itself, or what it stirs in us, but because of who it came from.

Unboxing our perceptions of how God demonstrates His love and what legitimate reactions to an encounter with His love are, helps us to realise that God is showing us His love all of the time, in so many different ways.

What would it look like for each of us to be free to recognise how God is demonstrating His love for us, moment by moment?

To have a church where every genuine response to an encounter with His love is not just welcomed, but encouraged?

---

[5]. It is worth noting that it is highly unlikely that God speaks to us in only one way. We can be assured that we can all hear His voice through Scripture, and confident that He will use many other moments and events of life to communicate with us.

The Truth

Every word that Jesus spoke is truth.

Every thing that Jesus did is true.

But both of those statements are true only because Jesus is the Truth.

Our primary calling as Christians is not to discover and retain all of the truths that Jesus taught and practiced. Our aim is not to *comprehend* truth.

Our life's objective is to discover, and to become increasingly acquainted with, the person who *is* the Truth.

I firmly believe that if we focus ourselves on the single-minded aim of knowing Jesus more, we will discover all the truth we need for our lives, and a lot more besides.

This does not mean that we disregard truths we hear or read, but it does mean that we use those as signposts to point us back to the one who is Truth itself.

Just as Jesus' demonstrations of love come from the fact that He is love, so every truth is found in Him because He is the Truth.

Knowing that Jesus Himself is the Truth, has to affect how we view Scripture.

For Scripture tells us all about truth, it leads us to truth and speaks only of truth, but it is not the Truth:

> *You search the Scriptures because you think that in them you have eternal life; and it is they that bear witness about me, yet you refuse to come to me that you may have life.*
> JOHN 5.39-40 ESV

Is not the point of Scripture that it is not all about the Scr

Do the Scriptures not shout at us to look beyond then uncontainable by them?

Let me reaffirm the classic, orthodox Christian belief that the Bible carries the full authority of God. It is God's word, inspired by the Spirit. It is wholly good, perfect, and true.

Scripture must not, and indeed cannot, be divorced or separated even one centimetre away from the Father. They belong together.

Scripture is perfect in its expression of God, speaking wholly of Him, unflawed in its descriptions, un-rivalled in its authority, and accurate in its every word.

Hidden in Scripture are more truths about God than we could ever imagine.

Scripture is the framework upon which we are to hang, and by which we are to assess, every encounter with God, every revelation, and every word we believe He has spoken.

Scripture is the scale upon which every aspect of the Christian life is weighed and tested.

And it is because of this high value of Scripture that we must remind ourselves that Scripture is not God Himself.

That is like claiming that a wedding invitation is the wedding.

An invitation gives you a flavour and an anticipation of the event to come. Its purpose is to speak only of the event, to represent the event well, and to create an appetite for the event.

But it is not the event.

No, it is the invitation.

Scripture is the invitation, Jesus is the party.

Scripture is essential in our lives. It is often used by God to lead us, direct us, help us, inspire us and correct us. It communicates His love for us, telling the story of His relentless pursuit of getting us back into relationship with Him.

But He gave us the Scriptures so that we can know that He is still alive, that He is still with us and that He still walks, talks and moves around us.

He gave us the Scriptures so that we know that we can know Him.

So let us open our eyes to the fact that Scripture longs for us to know the Truth.

The fully alive person of Jesus Christ.

The Life

Unsurprisingly, we now come to talk about the third statement that Jesus uses in *John 14.6*, that He is the Life.

It can be so easy to see what we *do* as the heart of our Christianity.

But whatever the activities—be it pursuing a dynamic community, seeing the kingdom come in the workplace, or praying for the sick to be healed—they are not the heart of Christianity, nor what makes the life of faith so vibrant.

It is Jesus Himself who is the Life of Christianity.

If we want to discover true life, we must realise that it is to be found within the person of Jesus.

Of course community, evangelism, prayer and sung worship are all things we are called to pursue, and God reveals Himself to us as we do so. However, it is not those things in and of themselves that makes us come alive, but God Himself.

If we feel that the life within our church, small group, or even within our own personal walk of faith, is anything short of full, taking on extra activities is not always the answer.

Let us instead look to Jesus and allow Him to direct our steps. He may ask us to do various things, but unless He is leading us, we will not experience life in all its fullness; we will just find a mere shadow.

So as we reflect on the Gospel, the Good News of Jesus Christ, let us primarily seek the reality of Jesus Himself.

As with Anthony, let us ask God to meet with us, to reveal Himself to us, and let us search for Him with all our hearts. Whenever God is hiding, He only ever does so to give us the joy of finding Him.

God has laid before us the greatest invitation of all time.

To know Him—the Father, the Spirit, and the Son.

The Son who is Himself the Way, the Truth, and the Life.

That Keeps Getting Better

So to the second half of this chapter's title, and indeed the book's.

From God's perspective the Gospel is not changing.

Jesus is already fully Jesus. He will never change. [6]

---

6. *Hebrews 13.8.*

In that regard, the Gospel is not getting better. It is impossible for it to get better because it is impossible for God to get any better than He already is.

However, we do not have all of the understanding about God that He does.

We do not yet know Him fully.

God will continually be showing us more of Himself until He comes again.[7]

As I've said in this chapter already, Jesus Christ is the Good News. The very person we have entered into relationship with *is* the Gospel.

As we walk with Jesus, He unveils to us more and more of Himself, and of His glorious nature. As we grow in our acquaintance with Him, we become increasingly aware of His goodness.

We see how amazing He is in ever-increasing measure.

From our perspective then, as people becoming ever more acquainted with the wonders of the person of Jesus, who is Himself the Good News, it seems like the Good News keeps getting better.

The remaining 11 chapters of this book explore areas of my life where witnessing the person of Jesus in increasing ways has made me feel like the Good News has kept on getting better.

Through seeing more of Christ, God has liberated me more than I thought possible. He has excited my heart for Him more than I ever expected, and He has continually amazed me with how He works, and how His Spirit can enable me to live.

---

7. *1 Corinthians 13.12.*

I firmly believe that God wants each of us to see more and more of Him.

Seeing more of God means that we encounter His love, because we cannot truly see God without seeing His love, and encountering His love means that we become who we were made to be;

Liberated lovers of God.

On this journey of seeing more of God, and being increasingly freed by God, I have been moved beyond words at how good God is, again and again.

As you read this book, my hope is that you will see God many times. I hope He will use my words, the stories of Him working in my life, to reveal more of Himself to you.

Whatever God shows you, puts His finger upon and speaks to you about, is for your good, because of His love for you.

All you need to do is intentionally invite Jesus to do with you as He wants, allowing Him to kindle a deep, true and passionate love for Him inside of you, as you witness Him revealing Himself to you again, and again, and again.

Like unwrapping a present, layer after layer.

He will always be better than we think.

He is the Good News, and to us, He is the Good News that keeps getting better.

2. Seekers, Finders, Minders, Keepers

The Salmon And The Crow

Before the Sunday services in my previous church, as happens in many churches, a group of people, including the pastor, service leader, preacher, intercessors and worship team, would gather together to pray and listen to God for the service ahead.

It was during one of these prayer times that someone had a prophetic picture of a birds-eye view of a river from source to mouth.

In the picture there was a crow that flew straight from the source of the river to the mouth, and there was also a salmon that swam every meander of the river until it reached the mouth.[1]

The person who received the picture then began to explain what they believed God was saying through it.

They thought that there were individuals in the service who could see a God-given target or objective very clearly in their lives, represented by the mouth of the river.

These people thought it logical to go straight from where they were, the source, to the objective, the mouth, as the crow flies.

God, on the other hand, was asking them to be more like the salmon.

For the salmon in this picture followed the meanders of the river to the mouth, rather than trying to find a straight route like the crow.

This meant that the salmon sometimes made turns that appeared to take it in the wrong direction, and that the overall journey took much longer than if it had been travelling in a straight line.

We all made appropriate mid-prayer-good-prophetic-word-agreement-noises, prayed it in, and readied ourselves for the service ahead.

---

1. Let us forget for a moment that salmon are better known for swimming upriver!

Calling And Destiny

...derstand the 'call' on our lives, or our God given ...ily become insatiable for any Christian.

We seek God, wanting Him to reveal the plans He has for us, so that we can find direction for our lives. Then, when He has revealed some of those plans, we knuckle down and work out the most direct route to fulfilling them.

For some reason we have it in our minds that we stand at the starting line and when God gives us something to do, we thank Him, set our compasses and head off, navigating the way towards the finish ourselves.

We can place the responsibility for fulfilling God's call on our lives solely on our own shoulders.[2]

It's a dangerous way of thinking.

Believing that it's our responsibility to fulfil God's call on our life can be very damaging for us.

It can lead to a life where we feel pressured to achieve God's plan for us in our own strength, thinking He will be disappointed if we fail, and daunted by the fact that we often have no idea what His purpose for our life is!

We must remember that God is more passionate to fulfil His call on our lives than we are.

---

[2] When I talk of God's 'call' on our lives, I don't mean that God only has one thing for each of us to do. God's call for each of us is made up of many calls that come together to make His ultimate call. In being obedient to the many, day-to-day calls of God, we are building towards the fulfilment of the overarching call on our lives.

God is more able to fulfil His call on our lives than we are.

And God *wants* to fulfil His call on our lives more than we do.

When God shows us glimpses of our calling or destiny, He isn't revealing tasks He would like us to achieve by ourselves, He is showing us what He intends to do through us and with us.

Our responsibility is to agree with what God says He intends to do through us, not to try and do what only God can do!

He is like a chess player who doesn't just move the pieces, but asks the pieces for their permission to be moved. Our choice, to give Him permission to use us or not, dictates whether He will move us into the position He wants.[3]

He is always adapting His game strategy depending on whether His pieces choose to agree with the move He desires to make.

Imagine yourself to be a knight on the chessboard.

How incredibly daunting would it be if you had to decide all of your own moves and were ultimately responsible for the outcome of the match?

You can't see everything.

As a knight on the board, even if you know that the aim of chess is to checkmate the opponent's king, your method of doing that, given your incredibly limited perspective, probably isn't the best method out there.

Often in chess a knight is moved forwards, then backwards, even side

---

[3]. Of course God values us incomparably more than a chess-player values their chess pieces.

to side, before eventually, if all goes well, playing its role in checkmating the opponent's king.

God knows when to move us forwards, backwards, or side to side, fulfilling His perfect plan for our lives and His world.

We're not asking God to help *us* win *our* game of chess.

And neither is He asking *us* to win *His* game.

We're being invited to partner *with Him* in winning *His* game of chess.

If we try to fulfil our God-given calling our own way, we will end up missing the joy of God taking us His way, at His speed.

For a period in my life I found myself trying to force what I perceived my calling to be, to happen as soon as possible. I would make decisions through the lens of what would get me 'there' fastest. The choices I made and the conversations I had were all seen through that lens.

I became selfish for the sake of my 'calling'.

But the ways of God don't lead to selfishness, they lead to selflessness.

My attempts to fulfil God's call on my life subtly began to make me less and less like Jesus.

We must ensure that we desire to see God fulfil His call on our lives His way.

If that isn't our primary desire and we try to fulfil God's call on our lives our own way, even if it seems an incredibly logical and wise way, we will miss out on the true fulfilment of our destiny and, quite probably, miss experiencing the fullness of life.

So, how does God reveal His calling on our lives to us?

How does He intend to walk us towards our calling's fulfilments?

What is He asking of us?

It is time to re-understand calling.

Seekers

Re-understanding calling begins through grasping what it means to be a true seeker of God.

It begins with seeking God because all things flow from God and lead back to Him.

Every calling God gives will come from Him and is designed to lead back to Him. If we do not love seeking God, then we do not love where the call comes from, or where it is meant to lead.

If we do not truly delight in seeking the Father, then we do not really comprehend the nature of God's calling.

Seeking God means relentlessly searching for God until we see Him.

A seeker is not satisfied with seeing God just once. No, they are determined to see Him over, and over, and over:

> *Blessed are the pure in heart, for they shall see God.*
> MATTHEW 5.8 ESV

Whilst this verse promises that we will see God in eternity, I believe it is also a promise for us now, prior to Jesus' return.

Perhaps not in the sense that we will physically see God with our eyes[4], but true in the sense that we can meet with Him by His Spirit.

His Spirit that is fully Him.

If seeking God means relentlessly searching for God in order to continually see Him, then according to *Matthew 5*, seekers need to be pure in heart.

Because the pure in heart, *"shall see God"*.

If we are passionate about seeking and seeing God, then we must be passionate about having pure hearts, because the want to seek God is driven by the desire to see Him, and seeing Him is dependant upon having a pure heart.

We cannot obtain pure hearts ourselves; ultimately they are given to believers by God thanks to His grace. However, every Christian faces daily choices of whether to live according to the pure heart God has placed within them, or to not.

A pure heart is one that has one focus, a single foundation.[5]

If we want to know how to live faithfully to the pure hearts God has placed within us by His grace, then we can look to Jesus as our example.

We know that Jesus lived a pure life and was always in connection with God.

So what was the pure, single foundation of Jesus' relationship with God the Father?

Love.

---

4. But don't rule it out! Jacob got to wrestle with God—that is a pretty physical encounter. *Genesis 32.30.*

5. We will look at this more in chapter 5, *Fire Isn't The Absence Of Water.*

Jesus chose to be in relationship with the Father every second of every day, continually seeking to see Him, because Jesus was constantly in love with the Father.

And by 'in love', I mean it in its fullest sense; emotional feelings, committed, consistent, self-sacrificial choices, and unrelenting passion.

Jesus' calling was underpinned by, and dependent upon, Him maintaining that foundation of love for the Father.

Every other aspect of Jesus' relationship with His Father was built on this foundation. But the foundation was, and indeed still is, simply and purely love.

God was able to fulfil His call on Jesus' life, which was to atone for the sins of humankind through Jesus' willing sacrifice and make a way for humans to re-enter a posture of right standing and relationship with God, because Jesus maintained a foundation of love for the Father throughout His life.

This foundation of love meant that the Father could ask anything of Jesus and, no matter what the cost to Himself, Jesus would say yes.

Jesus didn't unswervingly seek God to gain anything for himself. Rather, He sought the Father because He was captivated by the splendour of God.

Let us look at marriage to understand this further.

A marriage will flourish if it is built on committed, emotional, self-sacrificing and passionate love.

If someone chose to get married mainly because they felt insecure without a spouse, then the foundation of their marriage would be the need for security. Or if they married chiefly because they were desperate to wear a lovely ring on their finger, their marriage would be built on nothing greater than a desire for flashy jewellery.

I'm not suggesting that we need to feel totally secure before we get married, or that we must ensure we do not get excited about the blessings of marriage, but what I am saying is that love must be the foundation upon which those other things are worked out and enjoyed.

Without addressing impure foundations, a person cannot fully enjoy marriage, and indeed, will not be able to have a totally healthy marriage.

The Bible tells us that marriage is a picture of our relationship with God.

There will be moments when we are incredibly aware of our need for God, or very attracted to the benefits of following Jesus. These moments are normal because we make mistakes, Jesus transforms us, and He is incredibly kind and generous towards us.

However, if we are in a relationship with Jesus principally because of the good things we get from it, we are missing the pure foundation;

Love.

Not a love that changes its allegiance whimsically, or a love that holds on begrudgingly, but a love that is determined to remain faithful to God, no matter the cost, because it has encountered Him and His love.

The beauty of this love being the ultimate foundation of our relationship with God, is that we, as imitators of Christ, cannot have a love for God unless we experience His love for us; and we cannot continue to grow in our love for God unless we continue experiencing His love for us![6]

---

6. 1 John 4.19.

If we want to become true seekers of God, then we need to ask ourselves the question;

"What is the foundation of my faith?"

For Jesus the answer would be love; and as it is for Jesus, so it can be for us.

As we begin our journey in re-understanding calling, let us cry out to God to show us His love for us again and again, so that our love for Him may continually grow and burn within us more fiercely every day.

As we encounter His love, we will be filled with a passionate desire to seek Him, just for the delight of being with Him.

And those who seek God with a pure heart, with a foundation of love, will find Him.[7]

The Easter Egg Hunt

Every Easter my Mum would hide a whole host of Easter eggs in our garden.

We five kids would then hare around looking for them until we found one of each type of egg. Eventually we would have all the eggs Mum had hidden for us and would begin tucking into them happily.

The last time I did one of these Easter egg hunts, I struggled.

With an air of frustration and an especially forlorn look on my face, due to a depressingly empty bowl, I turned to my Mum and she pointed subtly in a direction I should search.

---

7. *Matthew 7.7 & Proverbs 8.17.*

I was still unable to find the majority of my eggs, while my siblings had found nearly all of theirs.

I stomped up to my Mum on the verge of angry tears, complaining that I couldn't find my eggs. She was then a little more directive, suggesting I try underneath the trampoline, or in the jasmine.

The only reason my Mum hid the eggs was so that we could find them. She could have given us all of the eggs at the beginning of the day and told us not to eat them all at once.

It took her quite some time to hide the eggs, and it took her still more time in the afternoon helping us to find them. It would have been quicker for her just to give us the eggs at the start of the day!

What did she gain from this venture of concealment?

Well, apart from a regrettably rare moment of peace and quiet whilst we were all otherwise occupied, she really enjoyed seeing us looking for the eggs.

I find it fascinating that as a child on Easter day, if I had been offered a few small chocolate eggs then and there, or the same eggs but hidden for me to find, I would have chosen the hidden eggs every time.

Finders

Seek and you will find.
MATTHEW 7.7B ESV

The second step in re-understanding calling is to become a finder, because those who seek, will find.

A finder is a seeker who sees what God is revealing and hears what He is saying.

Every time we seek God, we do not always find the same side of Him. Depending on what He knows we need, and indeed want, He reveals different aspects of Himself to us[8]:

> *[Things are hidden temporarily only as a means to revelation]. For there is nothing hidden except to be revealed, nor is anything [temporarily] kept secret except in order that it may be made known.*
> MARK 4.22 AMP

God has not revealed everything of Himself to humanity yet. In fact, He is deliberately holding parts of Himself back.

This is not to spite us, but so that He can show us all things at the perfect time.

As we grow in our relationship with Him, with that foundation of true love, He uncovers Himself and shows us the infinite wonders of His persons.

Someone who truly loves God does not stop seeking Him. This enables God to reveal all things to those who continually seek Him.

What peace and life are available to us who have the chance to walk with God continually, thanks to the grace given through Jesus Christ; grace that invites and enables us never to part from God, resulting in us always being before Him, ready to receive whatever He gives, knowing His goodness is perfect, His timing exemplary, and that His motivation is pure love.

He entrusts His revelations to those who are pure in heart, because those with that foundation of love are trustworthy.

---

8. This does not mean He changes at all, just that in His wisdom He knows what to reveal of Himself when.

not because of an ability to judge the value of what aled to them based on their perceived worth of each ...n, but trustworthy because true seekers treasure anything God reveals to them solely because the one they loved showed them something.

A true finder doesn't actually mind what God reveals to them.

The value lies not in what is revealed, but rather in the fact that it was God who revealed it.

Valuing what God shows us, whatever it may be, means that God can reveal anything to us, knowing that we will take heed of what He shows.

If we value what God reveals for any reason other than because it was God who revealed it, we may miss profound truths that God is wanting to show us.

God's timing in revealing things doesn't always fit with our own logic.

But His timing always fits with His plans.[9]

When God reveals something to you, it is the most relevant thing for you in that moment, even if you can't understand how.

Sometimes He waits an uncomfortably long time before providing a solution to a problem, and at other times He gives us a solution to a problem that we aren't even facing yet!

I've frequently wrestled and struggled with different decisions and

---

9. It is true that people's disobedience can hinder God's plans, however, disobedience cannot stop God's plans reaching their fulfilment. Just as a river finds a way to flow around an obstacle, so God's purposes find a way around mistakes and errors. *Proverbs 19.21.*

problems because I've been focusing so much on the issue at hand, that I've missed seeing what God is showing, or hearing what He is saying.

My friend, Jessie, once had a decision to make about where to live and what to do at the end of the summer.

She spent days wrestling with God for an answer until her friend advised her to spend time seeking God just for the enjoyment of being with Him.

To go to Him with no agenda.

To be a seeker.

As soon as she laid down her 'right' for an immediate answer to her question, and just enjoyed being with God, it suddenly became clear what God was leading her to do.

She had been looking so hard for a solution that she had been missing the answer God had waiting for her!

Instead of just bringing our issues and questions before God, perhaps we could bring ourselves in the midst of our issues and questions before Him?

Remember that God *wants* to show us truths; He just knows when the perfect time to do so is!

Mark 4.22 tells us that *"nothing is hidden except to be revealed"*. This means that the *only* reason God is hiding things is so that He can show them to us at the perfect time.

He may reveal truths about Himself, or truths about us in light of who He is. He may show us where we have believed something that isn't true, or He may give us something to do with Him, or something to look after.

This is where true calling is born.

It comes from a seeker enjoying being with God and God then revealing something that He intends to do with them.

For those who seek, will find.

If you do not know what your specific call is, don't worry! Instead, delight in God. Enjoy being with Him, experiencing and responding to His love.

He will show you what His plans for you are in good time, or He may show you what He has already done through you.

Either way, it is Him who does the revealing.

You do not need to work hard to discover your purpose. It is hidden within God, and you can trust that He will bring His purposes to pass in and through you as you live a life of delighting in Him.

So what do you do when God reveals something to you?

What is the next step in re-understanding calling?

Minders

> *He said to them, be careful what you are hearing. The measure [of thought and study] you give [to the truth you hear] will be the measure of [virtue and knowledge] that comes back to you—and more [besides] will be given to you who hear.*
> MARK 4.24 AMP

When God has revealed something to us it becomes ours to either mind well, or to cast aside. God always wants us to take heed of what He reveals, and allow it to take root within us.

When Jesus tells His disciples in *Mark 4.24* to be careful about what they are hearing, He is not talking about abstaining from unwholesome talk.

He is encouraging them to truly take to heart the truths that He has given to them.

This is why it is so important to value truths because it is God who is saying them, instead of valuing them for any other reason.

Often to understand a revelation from God, we must choose to listen to it and value it, even though we may not yet comprehend it. Through choosing to pay attention to the revelation, we allow it to be planted in our hearts, and over time it grows and flowers into something we can understand.

If we don't initially value a God-spoken truth because we don't understand it, we will miss out on a huge proportion of what God wants to show us.

Psalm 1 demonstrates this point:

> *His delight and desire are in the law of the Lord and on His law (the precepts, the instructions, the teachings of God) he habitually meditates (ponders and studies) by day and night.*
> PSALM 1.2 AMP

The Psalmist is describing what it means to be a minder of God's revelations.

Do you see?

The Psalmist's delight is in the word of God—He loves God speaking! He takes what he hears from God and thinks about it, meditating continually on it—planting it in his heart.

Through delighting in what God says, we grow in our understanding of His word.

Any word from God cannot be fully understood unless it is nurtured within an intimate relationship with God.

As we will see in the next 2 sections, through meditating on what God has said to us, we allow the revelation to grow to maturity within us and bear its fruit.

A person who delights in God (a seeker), hears what God says (a finder), and looks after what they hear (a minder), until it comes to maturity.

The Surprised Farmer

One of my favourite parables Jesus told is about a surprised farmer:

> *The Kingdom of God is like a man who scatters seed upon the ground,*
>
> *And then continues sleeping and rising night and day while the seed sprouts and grows and increases – he knows not how.*
>
> *The earth produces [acting] by itself – first the blade then the ear, then the full grain in the ear.*
>
> *But when the grain is ready and permits he sends forth [the reapers] and puts in the sickle, because the harvest stands ready.*
> MARK 4.26-29 AMP

The seed the farmer sows represents a truth revealed by God.

The planting represents the man taking it to heart – truly *hearing* what God has said to him.

Then, just like in *Psalm 1*, he keeps an eye on it night and day, watching over the word God has given him. He meditates on, and minds, God's word.

However, isn't it fascinating that the farmer doesn't *do* anything to the seed.

He watches and waits.

He looks at it.

But he doesn't touch it.

He doesn't try to force the seed to fruit.

Seeds are *meant* to grow into something, that's what they are designed to do!

Revelations from God are *designed* to bear fruit in our lives, we just need to wait and watch.

In the same way, callings are designed to reach their fulfilment. We get to stand amazed as God grows His calling through us until it is complete!

Don't try to force fruit.

If we are genuinely taking the revelations of God to heart out of love for Him, having faith in what He has said, they *will* bear fruit in our lives.

The joy of minding revelations from God is that they surprise us as they continue to grow inside us, changing us to become more like Jesus.

We get to be delightfully surprised at the work of God in us, because it is Him doing it, not us.

No matter what God has revealed to you, task or truth, He intends to bring it to maturity through you and in you. Your responsibility is to think about it, meditate on it, and believe it.

You are to be faithful with what God has given you, but it is *His* responsibility to make it bear fruit.

Don't try to rush the process; growth takes time.

Lay the growth of God's seeds into His hands (where they belong), knowing that He will bring them to fruition at exactly the right time.

And in the mean time, watch intently all that He is doing, minding all that He has said.

Keepers

His delight and desire are in the law of the Lord and on His law (the precepts, the instructions, the teachings of God) he habitually meditates (ponders and studies) by day and night

And he shall be like a tree firmly planted [and tended] by the streams of water, ready to bring forth its fruit in season; its leaf also shall not fade or whither; and everything he does shall prosper [and come to maturity].
PSALM 1.2-3 AMP

Verse 3 of *Psalm 1* lays out what will happen to someone who is a minder of a truth God has given them.

The Psalmist speaks of a faithful steward of God's revelation becoming like a tree secure in its place, ready to bear fruit in due season.

It is just like the parable of the farmer in *Mark 4*, where Jesus tells His disciples that at the right time the farmer reaps the harvest from the seed he sowed.

As I've already said, if we are good minders of the words and revelations of God in our lives, then they will come to maturity, and we will see the fruit.

And when these words do bear fruit, we get to reap the harvest.

We get to revel in and enjoy the fruit of the word of God. Our lives become more whole, free and fun, as God's words grow in us and change us.

Through the process of being a seeker, a finder and a minder, we see things from God come to fruition through, in and around us.

This is what we get to keep.

We get to keep the story and the testimony of what God has done.

We get to keep the personal transformation that comes from Him growing His purposes within us.

And we get to hold onto the sweet knowledge of Him that He has given us along the way.

As we reflect on that which God has brought to maturity in us, there is no doubt that God will want us to tell others of the amazing things that He taught us. He will want us to pass on all He did in us to those around us, so that they may go through the seeking, finding, minding and keeping process themselves.

Yet having authority to speak into other people's lives, and having words that people really desire to hear, are not the greatest rewards from this process.

The most valuable thing we get to keep is the ever-unfolding, deep, intimate and real knowledge of God Himself.[10]

---

10. *Philippians 3.10 AMP*

The result of the seeking, finding, minding and keeping journey is meant to be a fiercer, hungrier and more passionate desire to seek God:

> *Many waters cannot quench love, neither can the floods drown it. If a man were to give all the goods of his house for love, he would be utterly scorned and despised.*
> SONG OF SONGS 8.7 AMP

And so the cycle continues.

The Technicolour Coat Man

The story of Joseph is one about a seeker, finder, minder and keeper.

However, his route to seeing his destiny fulfilled was not a straightforward one. His journey was long and winding.

In his early years, Joseph demonstrated how not to 'mind' a calling well; but later in his life, through allowing God to teach him through his mistakes, Joseph also shows us how to 'mind' a calling very well.

Joseph felt God reveal his destiny to him in a dream, which included his brothers bowing down to him and him ruling over them.

When God first revealed this to Joseph, Joseph tried to make the destiny happen the next day. He took the responsibility to fulfil his calling onto his own shoulders.

However, in spite of Joseph's poor handling of God's revealed call, God graciously weaved and twisted circumstances to achieve His purpose.[11]

---

11. I do not believe that it was God's plan for Joseph to be sold into slavery, or thrown into a well. However, God used the outcome of young Joseph's arrogance to teach him, shape him and prepare him for all that was to come.

Just as a river finds a way around an obstacle in its path, so G
work His plans around our mistakes, redeeming our errors as He gc

Joseph's brothers decided to cast him into a well, and then sold him as a slave into the powerful household of Potiphar. Then, just when his destiny seemed to be coming true and he was growing in favour and recognition in that house, he was thrown into prison on a false charge made by Potiphar's wife because Joseph had refused to sleep with her.

By the time Joseph faced Potiphar's wife, he was a very changed man.

He could have slept with her to remain in a position of authority.

But he didn't.

He ran.

His love of God had become greater than his desire to fulfil his destiny.

He probably knew that running from Potiphar's wife would only lead to trouble, but he wouldn't sacrifice his integrity before God!

Eventually though, he was released from prison and promoted to be Pharaoh's right hand man.

Joseph's story is not one of going straight from A to B as the crow flies.

You could say that when he ended up in prison, it looked as if he was moving in the opposite direction from his calling.

God took him on a windy route to fulfil the call He had on Joseph's life. Yes, Joseph caused some of those twists and turns early on because he failed to steward God's revelation to him well, but even when Joseph made fantastic decisions that God delighted in, the route still wasn't straightforward!

step-by-step faithfulness to God, all because of a [...] for God, God established Joseph as Pharaoh's right [...] brothers did indeed come to kneel before him.[12]

[...] n learn from Joseph, was that even when he was [...] place of responsibility that looked like the fulfilment of his calling, he had to be willing to give it all up if that's what it took to stay true to God.

Walking in the fulfilment of our calling need never be more important that being faithful to God.

What would Joseph have missed out on had he continued to try and fulfil God's call his own way?

How could Joseph's story have been different if he hadn't 'minded' God's revealed call poorly in his younger years?

What would have happened if Joseph hadn't journeyed the meanders of the river?

The Salmon And The Crow

Let us return to the story of the salmon and the crow in their quest to find the river's mouth.

Which are we?

As God reveals great things to us that He desires to do with us and through us, we have to remember the salmon.

In the journey of seeing God's call on our lives fulfilled, we must vow to be led by the river of the Spirit, not the air of our own understanding.

---

12. Read the full story of Joseph in *Genesis, 37 & 39 —47*.

Let us choose to follow God's lead.

I have no doubt that sometimes God will lead us in the opposite direction to the one we thought we ought to be going in.

He sometimes asks us to travel more slowly than we desire, sometimes far more quickly.

But this one thing I know; if we remain faithful seekers of God, then God will achieve all that He intends to achieve through and in us.

Sometimes man's disobedience and sin can delay God's plans from coming about, however, even if God's chosen person for a given task rebels against Him, He will find a way to fulfil it through another.

For example, take King Saul; he did not remain faithful to God and so God could not fulfil His designed destiny for Saul through Saul. However, Saul's destiny to be a godly king of Israel could be, and eventually was, fulfilled through another – King David.

Even if others oppose God's work in our life, we must be confident in the knowledge that God can work around it.

How will He create an alternative route?

We do not always know.

But we do not need to know.

If we live seeking Him because we love Him, taking notice of what He is showing, not what He isn't, pondering the things He shows us in our hearts and enjoying the ever increasing relationship we get with Him thanks to the process, we will be able to follow God's path for us and God's route to fulfil His calling on our lives.

With that as the invitation, why would we say no?

3. Leaning On Nothing Until It Holds You Up

We Still Have To Swim!

As we follow God's plans for us, even when they take us in surprising directions, He calls us to commit all of our effort into swimming in the direction He is leading us.

Like the salmon from the last chapter, we don't simply let the flow of the river take us; we get to swim with the current of God's purposes.

Whether He is taking us in a direction we understand or not, we are invited to throw all of ourselves into following His lead.

In the eternal sense, the river will always reach the mouth whether we swim or not. God's eternal plan will unfold—Jesus will return and God's kingdom will be established on earth in its entirety.

But we can speed that happening through our agreement with God.[1] The river will always reach the mouth, but we can affect how fast!

God invites us to become His partners in seeing aspects of His coming kingdom here, on earth, now.

As we put our effort and passion into agreeing with God, He establishes His kingdom in, through and around us.

We may well have become used to the notion of 'the now and the not yet' in the Christian world.

It rolls off the tongue.

The 'now' of seeing aspects of God's kingdom breaking through into our world today, and the 'not yet' of acknowledging that His kingdom

---

[1] *2 Peter 3.11-12.* When Peter says, *"What sort of people ought you to be in lives of holiness and godliness, waiting for and hastening the coming of the day of God,"* he implies that the way God's people live can hasten *"the coming day of God"*, which is when Jesus will return.

will not be unveiled in its entirety until Jesus returns.

Rightly, the 'not yet' is used to explain why suffering, evil and pain still exist, and how we can understand disappointments and hurts.

The danger arises when this causes us to shy away from believing that God wants to establish vast swathes of His kingdom on earth through us in our lifetime 'now'.

When Jesus asked His followers to pray for God's kingdom to come[2], He neither specified nor implied that there was a limit to how much of His kingdom God wanted to give.

The Lord's Prayer was given to help Jesus' disciples shape their praying while still on earth, not to save until Jesus returned!

That means that the disciples were taught to pray for God's kingdom to come on earth whilst they were still alive.

And as He taught them, so He teaches us.

The 'now' of the coming of God's kingdom to earth is the solution to the anguish of the 'not yet'.

Instead of thinking that we should shrug our shoulders with a sigh of 'not yet' when faced with an unanswered prayer, let us run to God and petition Him for the 'now'!

The Spirit has been given to us to empower us to endure all things, disappointments, disasters and pain, so that we can contend for God's kingdom to come even in the midst of hardship.

Surely we have not reached a point where we have asked God for too much of His kingdom to come on earth?

---

2. *Matthew 6.10.*

I believe God would love to bring about far more of His kingdom on earth in our lifetimes than we ever dreamed of.

It is breath-taking to consider what God would love to establish through us agreeing with Him by being seekers, finders, minders and keepers.

God wants to bring His kingdom to earth through His people agreeing with Him not because He is unable to do it by Himself;

He is God.

He can do whatever He wants.

He would just rather not work alone.

It is His will, His joy and His delight to work in partnership with His people. When we agree with Him in the smallest thought or the largest action, we are playing our part in establishing heaven on earth.

This is why in the Lord's Prayer of *"Your kingdom come"*, is followed immediately by *"Your will be done."*[3]

How does God's kingdom come?

Through God's people agreeing with Him for His will to be done in every situation; whether His will is for a loud declaration to be made, a bold prayer of faith said, or a silent act of generosity offered, and everything in between.

When we pray for God's will to be done, we are saying a resounding, *"Yes!"* to whatever is in His heart to happen.

Our agreement releases His purposes.

---

3. *Matthew 6.10.*

And the key to this purpose-releasing agreement is faith, because faith enables us to agree with God even when He asks us to agree with things that we cannot yet see.

He can make what appears to us the craziest of promises, or say what seems to be the most ludicrous of statements, and yet faith enables us to agree with Him.

Think of Mary agreeing with God that she was to be pregnant with His Son!

Through faith, Mary is able to agree with God and walk into God's purposes for her.

In this chapter I want to look at the topic of faith because faith enables agreement, and agreement enables God's kingdom to come, and God's kingdom is what we have been called to usher in while still living on earth.

Before I do this, however, I want to look further at why agreeing with God is so significant.

If faith enables us to agree with God for His unseen kingdom to become seen amongst us, then the significance of faith lies within its ability to facilitate agreement.

The Power Of Agreement

Do two walk together unless they have made an appointment and have agreed?
AMOS 3.3 AMP

God has always given human beings choice.

Choice to agree with Him, or not.

Amos 3.3 explains that we cannot walk with God unless we agree with Him.

Jesus' walk with the Father was unbroken because His agreement with the Father was unbroken.

In Eden, God planted the tree of the knowledge of good and evil and told Adam and Eve about it so that they had the opportunity to choose to agree with Him.

Agreement cannot exist without choice, because unless agreement is chosen it is not truly agreement.

We know how much God values giving humankind the ability to choose to agree with Him by what it has cost Him.

What did it cost God to put the tree of the knowledge of good and evil in the Garden?

Because of the choice our ancestors made, it cost Him the life of some of His creation to cover our nakedness, it cost Him the perfection of His world, and it cost Him communion with us. Yet all of these are mere shadows compared with the cost God had to pay to put it all right again, sending Jesus Christ to His death.

There could be no higher cost.

And He would only have paid the highest price for something He values most highly.

When God planted the tree of the knowledge of good and evil in the Garden of Eden, He did not do so wanting to send His Son to His death. However, knowing what Adam and Eve would do, and what it would cost Him to undo their mistake, He still chose to plant that tree.

Putting the tree of the knowledge of good and evil in the Garden of Eden cost God Jesus' life.

Could God's immense value of His people having the freedom to choose Him be any clearer?

In contrast, the Devil wants to enslave us – to remove our ability to choose God. But Jesus sets us free to restore our chance to respond to God and choose Him again.

God is passionate about us having choice, and one of the reasons for this is that choice enables agreement.

And agreeing with God means we can walk with Him.

If agreement is something that God values so highly, how can we consistently choose to agree with Him?

If we look at the Trinity, we see three persons in total agreement all of the time. So much so that They are One as well as Three. Each member of the Trinity could choose to disagree at any moment, but They don't, and They won't.

Why do the members of the Trinity always choose to agree with each other, and how do They live in total harmony?

Because They love each other.

You see, the key to unbroken agreement is love, and the result of unbroken agreement is power.

It would be easy for us to try and consistently agree with God for the power that it brings. Seeing God's power in our lives is understandably something we desire, but that desire is not the key to consistent and unbroken agreement with God.

Jesus' agreement with God resulted in the most powerful life ever lived. Yet Jesus did not agree with God so that He could be powerful, or so that others could experience God's power.

Jesus agreed with God because He loved God.

Simple as that.

Wanting to see God's power in our lives is not wrong, it just isn't the reason that God designed us to choose Him.

Agreement is important because it is the means by which God has chosen to release His power and purposes into the world.

But agreement was designed to be a choice flowing from love.

He enjoys pure, loving relationships so much that He wants to share everything with His children.

He has made every spiritual blessing available to those who are in relationship with Him.[4]

We don't deserve it, but it isn't about whether we deserve it or not.

It's about how God wants to do things.

If He wants to work with us, then let us joyfully accept the grace of God that enables us to join His plans and activities.

Not our will, but His.

We need to remember that.

Humanity's agreement with God is the way in which God has ordained His kingdom to come to earth. At times, when we cannot yet see what God has promised, we need faith to keep on agreeing with Him.

Faith is the key to this purpose-releasing agreement because faith

---

4. *Ephesians 1.3.*

enables us to agree with God even when He asks us to agree with things that we cannot yet see.

So how do we become people of faith, enabling us to be people of unbroken agreement?

The Waltz

At mine and Rebekah's wedding reception there came the moment when everyone gathered around the dance floor for our first dance.

Contrary to rumour, we hadn't devised a routine, or taken lessons to ensure smooth gliding around the floor to wow the guests.

We improvised.

Admittedly, it was a slow song, which no doubt made it easier.

But the problem, as Rebekah tells me, was that it was very hard to predict where I was going to move my feet next.

Apparently, I had a little knack of deciding at the very last minute where my leading foot was going to land, giving her no warning of when it was going to move, or how quickly.

So valiantly did she follow my lead that I came away with the slightly misguided belief that I'd nailed it.

Midway through the song, other couples joined us to dance. We looked over to my parents who were waltzing across the other side of the dance floor.

My Mother didn't appear to have the same trouble following my Father's lead as Rebekah did mine. He let her know where he was going by beginning to move in plenty of time and not doing something completely random.

Much as I enjoy reminiscing about my wedding, there is a point in that I wish to draw out.

Faith

God is the most gracious of dance partners.

He leads in such a manner that we have the opportunity to position ourselves for what He is about to do next.

Sure, sometimes He does His own thing and just takes us with Him, sweeping us off our feet. But on the whole, He lets us know first.[5]

He gives us a chance to get ready for His next move.

Faith is what enables us to believe God when He tells us He is going to move somewhere before He has actually moved there.

When a dancer senses that their partner is about to move, they ready themselves in anticipation of that move.

If they don't, the dance falls apart.

It's the same with faith.

It is about positioning ourselves based on something God has said will happen in such a way that if it didn't come to pass, we would fall over.

So often we feel God say something to us but want to wait to see it happen before we let ourselves believe it.

Faith doesn't work like that!

---

5. *Amos 3.7 & John 16.13.*

repare for what He is going to do.

e, we are hindering the dance.

ing the things He desires to do.

I've heard it taught that faith is about putting ourselves in situations where we *"need God to show up"*, pushing ourselves *"out of our comfort zones"*, and making ourselves *"take risks"*.

But faith is a response to God, a gift from Him.

Faith is not obtained through our ability to push ourselves.

Faith may well lead us to put ourselves in a situation where we feel outside of our comfort zones, but without God leading us there, forcing ourselves to *"take risks"* is just an attempt to manufacture faith ourselves.

In order to position ourselves for what God has said He will do, we must believe it is actually going to happen. Without that heartfelt belief, we are like a dancer who doesn't trust that their partner is going to go the way they said they would.

God is asking us to believe in what He says so that He can achieve all that He wants to achieve with us.

People of faith believe that God is able to do what He says He will do.

They trust that what He says He will do, He will do.

And they wait for what He says He will do to unfold, in His perfect time.

Belief, trust and patience.

Who's Driving?

I have given you every place on which the sole of your foot treads, just as I promised to Moses.
JOSHUA 1.3 ESV

Before we move on to belief, trust and patience, I want to mention briefly that sometimes God allows us to take more of a lead in the dance.

When Joshua leads Israel into the Promised Land, God says that He will have already given Joshua any land on which he walks.

Within God's will, represented by the Promised Land, Joshua could choose where to go, knowing that God had given him that land. Not for Joshua's own gain, but for the furthering of God's kingdom, for the benefit of God's people.

Sometimes the will of God is a narrow path that requires us to do only what God says, and at other times the will of God is like a vast expansive garden in which He invites us to choose where we would like to go and explore.

He gives us choices.

Not trick choices, but actual choices where more than one answer is good!

We don't always need to ask God about every little thing we intend to do, because when we are living in a time where His will for us is there to be explored, not just followed, we can carry an assurance of His approval over us in whatever choices we make.[6]

I've written more about this in two later chapters, *Permission Or Blessing?* and *Resetting Default Settings*.

---

6. As long as the choices are in line with God's character and calling.

Father Abraham

The story of Abraham is nothing short of inspirational.

God tells Abraham that he is going to have as many descendants as there are stars in the sky.[7]

He's told this when he is 100 years old and his wife is in her 90s.[8]

He's told this when he doesn't have any children.

Safe to say, it doesn't look particularly likely.

Abraham has a choice at this moment. God is telling him one thing, logic is telling him another.

God is telling him something seemingly unbelievable, yet asking Abraham to believe it.

In Scripture, we see that God has quite a habit of doing unbelievable things through ordinary people.

People like you and me.

The first step to being able to have faith to agree with God is to believe that God is able to do what He says He intends to do.

In Abraham's case, that God was able to give him and Sarah a child in their old age.

The heartfelt belief that God is able comes from knowing Him – knowing what He is like. If we find ourselves not believing that God is able, the answer is not to bury our head in the sand and pretend we

---

[7]. *Genesis 15.5.*

[8]. *Genesis 17.17.*

believe He is.

We just don't need to live like that!

Take a leaf out of Abraham's book; he didn't initially believe that he could have a son in his old age.

So did he just pretend to believe God's promise and crack on?

No!

He asked God if He was serious, and whether God realised how old he was.

It's through opening up to God about where we are struggling to believe that He is able, that He can speak to our hearts and reveal to us that He is!

Only time with God can make you truly believe He is able. You can't know how able He is if you don't know Him and if you haven't seen Him at work.

God is inviting us to see Him and to talk with Him; to experience for ourselves His ability, His wisdom and all the other wonders of His character!

Trust

Belief in God's ability must be married to a trust that God will be true to His word; that He will do what He says He will do.

It's no good believing that God *can* do something if we do not trust that He *will.*

that God promises Abraham many descendants is in how much time passes between *Genesis 15* and *16*, but *Genesis 16* starts with the fact that Abraham's wife, Sarah, hasn't yet given birth to a son and so she offers Abraham her servant, Hagar, to try and give Abraham an heir.

To Abraham, this seems the only way to turn God's promise into reality.

So he accepts.

Hagar gives birth to Ishmael, but Ishmael is not God's plan. Ishmael was Abraham and Sarah's attempt to fulfil God's plan.

Both Sarah and Abraham lost trust that God was going to do what God said He was going to do, and so they created their own way to begin fulfilling His promise themselves.

They took the responsibility for fulfilling God's promise in whatever way they could.

We must remind ourselves that if God says He intends to do something, He will do it!

We don't need to take the weight of God's work onto our own shoulders.

Eventually Sarah does become pregnant with Abraham's son, Isaac, and he is the one who God fulfils His promise to Abraham through.

Belief that God is able needs to be married to a trust that God is

---

9. Abraham and Sarah had different names before *Genesis 17* (Abram and Sarai) but I'm referring to them with their post *Genesis 17* names, as they're better known as Abraham and Sarah.

faithful, in order for us to be people of faith.

Trust Him no matter how unlikely His promises seem, and no matter how long He takes to act.

Patience

The passage of time after God has spoken and before He does what He said He would do, is one of the most common times our faith in God fulfilling His promises can be shaken.

So often we feel the crushing weight of time running out.

Our heads can be filled with accusations such as;

"I'm past my best."

Or;

"I've missed it."

When we begin to feel like time is getting away from us, we begin to doubt God, and we can begin to search for any fulfilment to His promises that we can find.

Like Sarah and Abraham, we try to find a way to help God out, which often compromises our own obedience.

If God has all of the wisdom, and He knows the best way for His plans to unfold, then what's the rush?

If God isn't rushing, I don't suppose we need to either.

Over and over in Scripture, we find people having to wait a long time for God's promises to be fulfilled, and then, when they do begin to be fulfilled, they happen very quickly indeed.

It is important to recognise that sometimes disobedience can cause a delay in a word from God coming to fruition. If in doubt, let us come before the Spirit honestly, and ask Him to reveal any disobedience within us. If we feel His finger rest on something, let us apologise quickly, let it go, and then continue to walk with God in confidence because of His grace.

Israel's disobedience and grumbling meant that they spent 40 years wandering in the desert waiting for the fulfilment of the promise of the Promised Land.

Then suddenly, God tells Joshua that they can go on in.[10]

If we truly believe that God is able, and trust that He will do as He says He will, then, no matter what happens in between, we will be peacefully content to go at the speed that God desires to go at.

We need to learn to be expectantly patient, knowing that God is able, and that He is faithful.

Mind The Gap

As I've just said, the most challenging time to believe and trust fully in God, is in the gap between when He says something, and when He does it.

It is easy to lose faith in the gap.

King David faced this gap many times in his life. After Samuel had anointed him King of Israel, many years passed before he was actually crowned. And although David had at least two chances to kill Saul, the King of Israel at the time who was standing in the way of the fulfilment of God's promise, David refused to compromise his integrity for the

---

[10]. God gives Joshua permission to enter the Promised Land in *Joshua 1*.

sake of his destiny.[11]

David's success lay in his ability to believe and trust in God for the fulfilment of His word when it looked like he was moving in the opposite direction from it.

David was expectantly patient for God to make good on His word:

> *[What, what would have become of me] had I not expected to see the goodness of God in the land of the living?*
>
> *Wait and hope for and expect the Lord; be brave and of good courage and let your heart be stout and enduring. Yes, wait for and hope for and expect the Lord.*
> PSALM 27.13-14 AMP

Verse 13 speaks of active waiting.

No faith is required to wait hopelessly.

That's called giving up.

David knew that holding onto his belief that God was going to fulfil His word enabled him to remain hopeful, faithful and to live in agreement with God, even in the gap.

If David hadn't remained hopeful in the gap, he would either have walked away from waiting and given up, or tried to seize the first thing that resembled the fulfilment of his calling.

Neither would have led to the true, life-giving fulfilment of his calling that God was preparing for him.

We know from reading other of King David's *Psalms* that he had

---

11. David's story of becoming the King of Israel can be found in *1 Samuel 16 – 2 Samuel 7*.

Lean On Nothing Until It Holds You Up

moments when he really didn't feel full of belief, trust or patience.

But each time he lost hope, David went into the presence of God to gain God's perspective again.

Through being a seeker of God, David remained wholly expectant that God would act in his lifetime.

It is normal for God to place such strong yearnings within us for the things He has promised that we weep and cry out in the days and years before their fulfilment. There will be moments when we feel down or disappointed that God's word hasn't yet been fulfilled, or that a truth in Scripture doesn't appear to be true for us at present.

But as we see from David, Abraham and other heroines and heroes of Scripture, the key to dealing with disappointments lies in being open with God in His presence. Only He can reinstall the true belief, trust and patience needed to be a person of faith.

And from being in His presence we will be filled with the knowledge that He is able, trustworthy and that His timing is perfect.

Love Works

If you love me, you will keep my commandments
JOHN 14.15 ESV

I hope that as you read this chapter, and all of the others in this book, you will see the thread that will continue to develop as this book progresses.

My dear friend Jon told me that God's plans depend on us depending on Him.

It depends on me depending on God.

Too often we have only looked at the first half of that statement, slowly becoming crushed and guilt-ridden by our inability to fulfil all of God's plans ourselves; by the pressure that comes from the belief that it 'all depends on me'.

Some have taken verses like *John 14.15* to mean that if we are serious about loving God, then we must make ourselves do all that He commanded; we must achieve for ourselves all He asks of us.

But what if Jesus was promising that if we love Him, we will naturally pursue all that He commands?

What if Jesus was making a promise to His disciples that if they remained truly in love with Him, they would find themselves doing the very things He commanded them to?

What if it all depends on us loving God?

What if love works?

The marvel of this is that my love for the Father actually comes from His love for me.

I can't love Him unless I am in His love—just like Jesus teaches in *John 15*.

We have an important choice to make that will impact everyone and everything.

Will we put ourselves before God, and allow Him to love us, without holding any part of ourselves back?

Perhaps, through allowing ourselves to be continually filled by the love of God, we will find ourselves walking just as Jesus Christ Himself walked.[12]

---

12. *1 John 2.6 & John 14.12.*

Leaning On Nothing Until It Holds You Up

Now faith is the assurance of things hoped for, the conviction of things not seen
HEBREWS 11.1 ESV

Hebrews 11.1 tells us that faith is believing that something is true before it is visible; believing so strongly in something that you lean your entire weight on it, even though you can't yet see it.

As we position ourselves based on what God has said will be, not what is, God's promises begin to form by His power and grace.

Each time God tells us of a move He is about to make, we have an invitation to position ourselves in anticipation of Him. Not a half-hearted anticipation, but a throwing of our entire mass in the assurance of His coming move.

For a moment it feels as though we have thrown ourselves onto nothing.

It appears that we are leaning on emptiness.

But suddenly God moves; He sweeps in and props us up.

Just as He said He would.

Just in time to hold us.

We will only believe, trust and wait for Him if we know Him.

We can only know Him if we see Him.

We will only see Him if we seek Him.

And we will only seek Him if we love Him.

Let us open our eyes and gaze on God so that we may receive the gift of faith that comes through seeing the God who is wholly faithful.

Selah.

(Pause, and calmly think of that)[13]

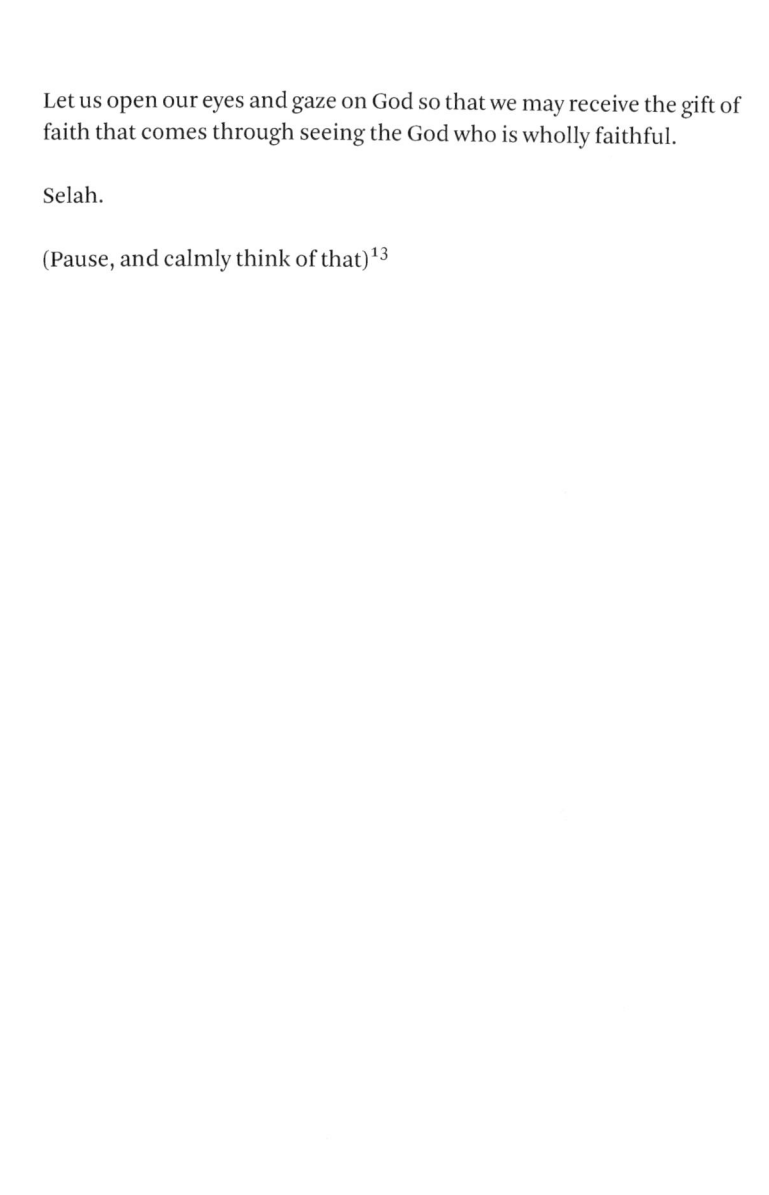

13. This is the Amplified Bible's definition of 'Selah'. For an example see *Psalm 3.2*.

4. TURNING SIN OUTSIDE IN

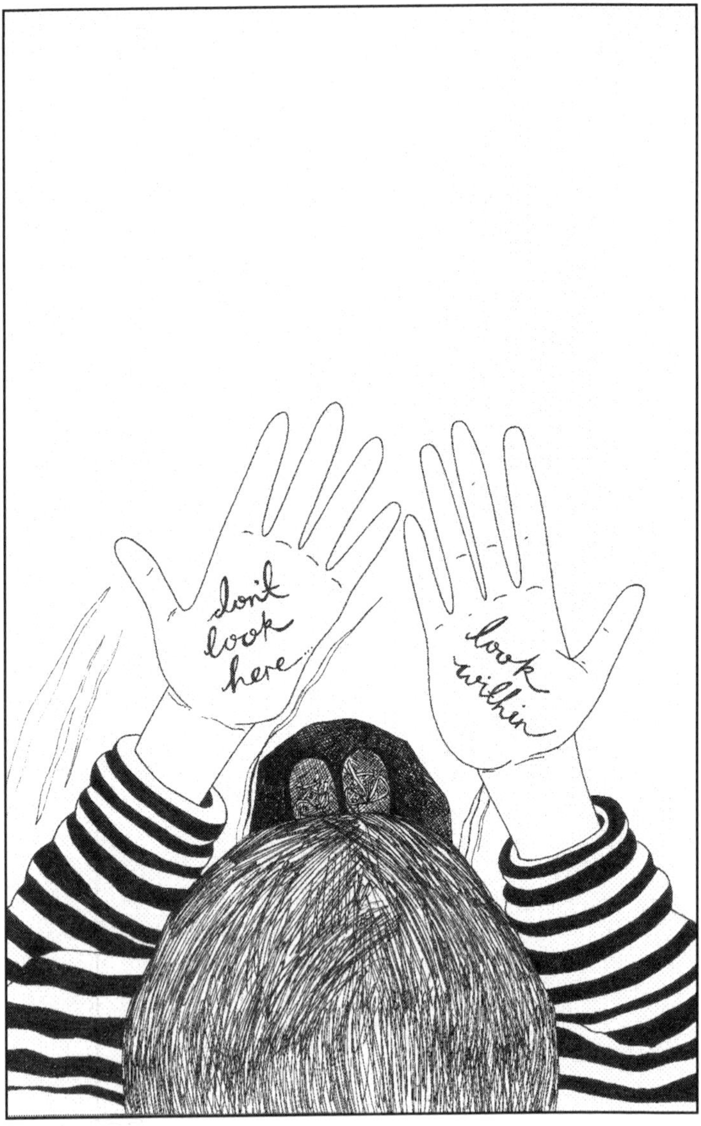
don't look here...
look within

What Is Sin?

The battle against sin is one of the most talked about topics in the Christian community. We want to know how to master it and how to be free from it; if we even believe we can be free from it.

I have heard sin defined in many different ways over the years. Most of the definitions were based on doing things that displeased God, or acting in rebellion towards God's rule and reign in my life.

In my opinion, neither of those definitions of sin do it justice.

They are the symptoms of sin, but they are not sin itself:

> *And He, when He comes, will convict the world about [the guilt of] sin [and the need for a Savior], and about righteousness, and about judgment:*
>
> *about sin [and the true nature of it], because they do not believe in Me [and My message];*
>
> *about righteousness [personal integrity and godly character], because I am going to My Father and you will no longer see Me;*
>
> *about judgment [the certainty of it], because the ruler of this world (Satan) has been judged and condemned.*
> JOHN 16.8-11 AMP

Just before the verses above from *John 16*, Jesus promises His disciples that it is better for them that He should leave, so that the Holy Spirit will come.[1] Then in *John 16.8-11*, Jesus says that the Holy Spirit will convict the world on three things; sin, righteousness and judgment.

---

1. *John 16.7.*

When Jesus says that the Holy Spirit is going to *"convict the world"*, it implies that the world has the wrong definition of sin, righteousness and judgment.

The world must have thought one way, and the Holy Spirit was coming to correct them and show them the right way.[2]

And Jesus gives us a helpful synopsis as to what the correct way of thinking about those three things will be.

According to Jesus in *John 16.9*, the correct definition of sin is that it is when *"they (people) do not believe in me"*.

The world thought that sin was when someone did something forbidden; yet Jesus tells His disciples that the correct understanding of sin is when someone does not have faith, or belief, in Him.

Jesus lets the disciples in on the secret; sin is all about not having faith in Him.

Both on the largest possible scale, but also the smallest. Not only does Jesus invite us to place faith in Him that will lead to an eternity with Him, but He also beckons us to have faith in Him in the midst of the smallest and most mundane day-to-day activities; to *continually* live by faith in Him.

The old way of understanding sin was all about breaking the rules, but the correct way of understanding sin, according to Jesus in *John 16.9*, is about whether we live from a position of faith in Jesus.

The law told people that certain actions were sinful, but Jesus tells His disciples that it is actually the miss-belief underpinning the action

---

2. In the NIV's translation of *John 16.8*, instead of the words *"convict the world about sin"*, it says, *"prove the world to be in the wrong about sin"*. This is why I believe the phrase *"convict the world"* can be translated into the phrase, *"to correct the world"*.

that makes it sinful.

Paul learnt this life-giving lesson from the Holy Spirit, as we can see in *Romans 14*:

> *For whatever does not proceed from faith is sin.*
> ROMANS 14.23B ESV

In the rest of *Romans 14*, Paul is addressing the question of whether believers can eat meat that has been sacrificed to idols.

In brief, he says that people needn't fear that such meat can have any power over them as a result of it having been used as a sacrifice to an idol. Jesus has power and authority over all things, so if the believers have faith in the cleansing power of Jesus, they can eat it.

However, Paul also says that some believers may not feel comfortable eating sacrificed meat, and that those who do feel happy eating the sacrificed meat should not force those who don't, to eat it.

His reasoning for this is that if someone is forced to do something that goes against a conviction they hold, they could be being led into sin.

Because anything that doesn't come from a place of faith in Jesus, is sin.

The Dinner Party

Picture the scene.

Rose and Albert are both sitting at the dining table with a lovely roast in front of them that their dear friends, Susie and Roger, have clubbed together to cook.

The meat has come from an animal used in a sacrifice to a pagan god. Susie, Rose and Roger feel very peaceful about eating the meat because they all believe in the authority of Jesus to cleanse all things, including the leg of lamb set before them.

Albert, however, is feeling distinctly uncomfortable with the whole ordeal.

But, not wanting to embarrass his wife, Rose, in front of their good friends, Susie and Roger, he decides to swallow his uncomfortable feeling along with the lamb.

If we press pause and ask the class who is sinning by eating the lamb from just observing them, it would be an impressive guess at best if someone chose Albert.

Why?

Because they're all *doing* the same thing.

They're all eating lamb.

Do you see?

In *Romans 14* Paul is telling the Roman church that there needs to be a transition in their understanding of sin. Instead of sin being primarily an external, action-based theology, it is actually an internal, faith-based theology.

Albert was *doing* the same as those around him, yet his internal conviction was different to theirs.

Susie, Roger and Rose all believed that God had cleansed the meat and so they were eating the lamb from a place of faith.

Albert did not believe that the meat was clean, and so was not living from a place of faith.

Anything that doesn't come from faith is sin.

Sin is about where an action comes from, not what the action is.

For too long some of us have believed that there is a list of actions that are 'sinful', without asking the question, *"Why?"*

Of course there are actions that will never proceed from faith, such as murder or adultery, but they are not sin purely because they appear on a 'sin list'.

They are sin because they are actions that will never come from a place of faith in Jesus!

They are some of the things the Spirit will never lead us to do.

When Paul wrote to churches forbidding them from doing certain things, he wasn't just banning certain actions; he was rebuking actions that were coming from impure motives. Paul knew that the things some of these churches were practicing were not coming from a place of faith in Jesus, and so he corrects them.

Not just so that they will amend their practices, but so that they will realise what is happening within their hearts.

Some of us have been teaching an unofficial law, telling people that there are some things that are objectively wrong without delving into the internal beliefs behind these 'banned' actions.

God's desire is for us to live by faith, not by laws.

This does not mean that God isn't passionate in His dislike of sin.

He hates it and could not be further from it, which is why He has done everything necessary to deal with it for once and for all![3]

---

3. *1 Peter 3.18.*

But the problem of sin that Jesus came to resolve was not one caused primarily by people 'breaking the rules'; it was one of relational distance caused by people living in rebellion to God in their hearts.

Surely the narrative of Scripture clearly shows that God desires us to have pure hearts towards Him, not just that we adhere to a set of regulations?

The regulations that the people in the Old Testament tried their upmost to follow, could not get them pure hearts.

These pure hearts that God so desires His people to have towards Him, are exactly what the sacrifice of Jesus has made available to us.

As we grow into these pure hearts, given solely by the kindness and graciousness of Jesus, we find that our actions and lifestyle begin to resemble that of Jesus'.

For every belief we have in our hearts works its way into our actions, our hands.

Whether it is a new, glorious belief in Jesus, or a belief in a lie from Satan, it will work its way out into what we say and do.

> *Faith without works is dead*
> JAMES 2.20 NIV

Faith and action have always been linked, and faith, no matter what it is in, always leads to works. If we think we can have faith in something without it affecting our actions and behaviour, we are mistaken.

For belief always leads to action.

If we find ourselves doing and thinking things that we don't believe are God's best for us, then let us ask the Spirit to explain our beliefs in that moment, asking Him to uproot and dispose of any beliefs that aren't based on the truth of the Gospel.

As we allow the Spirit to continually change our hearts, I believe we will see ourselves doing loving deeds.

Because faith in Jesus, leads to kingdom works.

And faith in a lie, leads to us doing things that reflect that lie.

The question is not, *"What are you doing?"*

It is, *"In what are you believing?"*

Heart To Hand

Blessed are the meek,
For they shall inherit the earth!

Blessed are those who hunger and thirst for righteousness,
For they shall be satisfied!

Blessed are the merciful,
For they shall receive mercy!

Blessed are the pure in heart,
For they shall see God!

Blessed are the peacemakers,
For they shall be called sons of God!
MATTHEW 5.5-9 ESV

Sometimes I feel like we try harder to imitate what Jesus did with His hands, than we do trying to imitate who He is in His heart.

If we want to see works similar to the works of Jesus coming from our hands, then we must understand who He is in His heart.

What does He value?

What are His priorities?

How does He work?

In the Beatitudes Jesus unveils what is on the inside of Him.

His heart.

He doesn't say that those who *demonstrate* meekness inherit the earth.

It's not those who *show* hunger for righteousness who will be satisfied.

Or those who *act* mercifully who will be shown mercy.

Nor those who *do* pure things.

Jesus is telling people to *become* different, not just to *do* differently, if they truly want to be like Him.

To further drive this home to the crowd listening to Him, Jesus talks about anger and lust being matters of the heart.

If you harbour anger in your heart towards another, you will be subject to judgement, because it is as if you physically harmed them, even murdered them.[4]

If you look at, or think about, a person lustfully, Jesus says you've committed adultery with them in your heart.

Jesus is trying to demonstrate to the crowd that righteousness is about your inside.

---

4. *Matthew 5.21-22 & 27-28.*

Your heart.

Where the law taught people not to do certain things in order to be righteous, Jesus explains that righteousness is actually to do with the state of the heart.

Let me reiterate that we cannot achieve this righteousness of heart by our own effort or resolve.

Scripture lays it plainly before us when it says that no one is good other than God[5], and that we've all fallen short of His righteousness through our rebellion.[6]

But this makes the righteousness on offer all the more outrageous.

God is the only one who is righteous, and yet He was willing to die to make it available to others who stood no chance of obtaining it for themselves.

Not only that, but this righteousness of heart is totally transformational for everyone who welcomes it.

A total transformation that works its way out to affect every little thing we do.

Our actions are a signpost to the state of our hearts.

John tells us in *1 John 1.6* that we cannot claim to have love within us whilst acting in an unloving way, and in the same vein, we cannot claim to be agreeing with the righteousness set within us by God's grace, if we are not acting righteously.

Because love leads to demonstrations of love, and righteousness leads to demonstrations of righteousness.

---

5. *Mark 10.18.*
6. *Romans 3.23.*

If we are truly being filled with God's love, it will be reflected in what we do. This need not make us try to act in a loving way to convince our hearts that they have been filled by God's love, but is an encouragement that God's transformation is not just an internal reality, but an all-consuming renovation that can been seen in the works of our hands.

The righteousness of God, unobtainable by man, has been gifted to those who believe in God, thanks to His grace, and the death and resurrection of God's own Son.[7]

This righteousness makes its home in our hearts along with the presence of the Spirit.[8]

Sin and righteousness are opposites that have always contested for the same property.

The heart.

If we believe that sin is just about what we do, when we do something we perceive to be sinful, our response will be to only address our actions so that we don't do the same thing again.

However, in light of the teaching of Jesus in *Matthew 5*, we know better.

Sin works its way from our hearts to our hands, our works. So instead of simply addressing what we do, we must look at our motivations and desires, trusting that a healthy heart will lead to healthy actions.

We get to look beyond trying to control what we do and seek to understand the fabric of who we are.

Why do we do what we do?

---

7. *Romans 5.9 & 2 Corinthians 5.21.*

8. *Romans 10.10 AMP & 1 Corinthians 3.16.*

How can we become like Jesus on the inside, not just

Upside-Down-Cake

When God taught me that sin originated from a lack of faith in my heart, it changed how I responded to bad decisions I made, and the bad habits I had.

Take the example of anger.

I always thought that to beat anger in my life I needed to suppress any anger I ever felt, which I took to mean avoiding any situation where someone annoyed me, or cutting short conversations that were starting to rub me up the wrong way.

You get the idea.

But if I did let my anger get the better of me, and it bubbled out onto some poor unsuspecting victim, after a suitable period of feeling guilty and sorry for myself, I would stringently try to not do it again. I would tell my accountability partner, vow to him and myself that I wouldn't do it again and, if I did, I would let him know what further precautionary action I would take.

Effectively, I was trying to manage my 'sin'.

We have to stop here and ask ourselves;

"Since when was life to the full merely a sin management program?"

Avoiding a situation where 'sin' may appear in our lives is like trying to hide a spot with make-up.

It doesn't remove the spot's presence; it just makes it less obvious to others, maybe even less obvious to us!

Turning Sin Outside In   86

we equate victory over sin as 'never doing something we think
be wrong'. And to ensure this, we try to avoid any situation where
temptation might arise.

We must stop thinking that being able to avoid making mistakes is
the pinnacle of sinlessness.

That is just avoiding the problem.

Of course it is good to not allow an emotion such as anger to master
us, but we don't have to settle for simply preventing ourselves from
doing something regrettable; we can ask the Spirit to heal, change and
restore our hearts so that anger never threatens to get the better of us.

When I look at the life of Jesus as portrayed by Scripture, I don't see a
man continually trying to make sure He doesn't sin. I don't see a man
who is continually making mental assessments as to whether He is
in a 'risky environment' or not; like how to make a good exit from an
'awkward situation' when a woman starts crying on His feet.[9]

I don't see a man who avoids being near people who might lead Him
to sin.

I don't see a man putting sin cover-up on.

I see a man who is so free and full of love for God that making
a decision, or doing something from a place outside of faith—
'sinning'—just didn't appeal to Him in the slightest.

Jesus was not spending His time on earth thinking about how not to
sin; His mind was consumed with pursuing the will of the Father.

The life of Jesus is an example to every believer of what is possible
through the grace of God and the power of the Holy Spirit.

---

9. *Luke 7.36-50.*

Please understand that I'm not proposing we all rush out and throw ourselves into the environments where we struggle the most! On the whole, God takes His time to transform our hearts, and then it takes more time still for this transformation to alter out actions.

But I long for us to see that it is possible for God to change our hearts so much that we no longer find *any* environment too much to bear.

That God can totally transform us.

Will there be temptation?

No doubt there will; but a faith and love for Jesus grown within us by God can far outweigh the most deceptively attractive temptation thrown at us from hell.

So how do we become like Jesus with regards to sin?

How do we become so consumed with faith that all else fades to nothing?

Self-Control

> *But the fruit of the Spirit is love, joy, peace, patience, kindness, goodness, faithfulness, gentleness, self-control; against such things there is no law.*
> GALATIANS 5.22-23 ESV

For me, the first step to understanding Jesus' notion of sin was to have my understanding of one particular fruit of the Spirit, self-control, corrected.

I had always thought that self-control was the key to living a life free from 'sin' because it enabled me to exert control over my actions, and I had believed that 'sin' was primarily about *doing* the wrong things.

If I could control myself so I didn't do something bad, I was winning against sin.

But what I discovered was that this understanding of self-control came almost entirely from my own effort; I found myself loathing and hiding the parts of me that I couldn't control, and becoming proud of the parts I could.

No fruit of the Spirit leads to self-loathing or pride, and no fruit of the Spirit comes from one's own strength.

So this notion of self-control was incorrect.

One morning my old mentor, Greg, was in the office preparing a sermon, when I walked in.

We often talked through each other's sermons and threw ideas around.

That day Greg had been thinking about the fruit of the Holy Spirit:

Love, joy, peace, patience, kindness, goodness, faithfulness, gentleness and self-control.[10]

Greg asked me why I thought we need the Holy Spirit to help us gain self-control?

He could understand why we needed the Holy Spirit for all of the other fruit, but not for this one.

Surely the whole point of *self*-control is that we should be able to control ourselves without anybody else's help?

Why do we need the presence of God to empower us to control ourselves?

---

10. *Galatians 5.22-23.*

We talked and laughed for a while, trying to find an answer, and we eventually stumbled upon the fact that perhaps it was because we weren't truly ourselves without the Holy Spirit's presence within us.

If self-control is about controlling oneself, then the only reason we would need another's presence within us to enable us to control ourselves is if we weren't truly us without them.

How can you control yourself if you're not yet you?

What I realised was that the Holy Spirit's presence inside of me is an integral part of me.

Without Him, I'm not the full me I was made to be.

As I reflected on this revelation, I became hopeful that I could finally have self-control. I understood that I wasn't fully me without the Holy Spirit, so now that I needed to be full of Him in order to be truly myself, surely I would have self-control and I could win in the battle of sin in my life once and for all?

Not quite.

Self-control isn't at the top of the Holy Spirit's priority list.

Galatians 5.22-23 tells us it's a fruit; by very definition it is a product of the Spirit's presence within us.

The aim, purpose and focus of the Holy Spirit is to lead us to the Father, teaching us everything that Jesus taught.[11] The Spirit does this by rooting us in the love of God and overwhelming us with His presence.

That is what it means to be filled continually with the Holy Spirit.[12]

---

11. *John 14.26.*
12. I've added 'continually' here because when Paul talks about being *(cont. on next page)*

The *by-product* of being filled continually with the Holy Spirit is that the fruit of the Spirit grows and flourishes within us.

Just like a healthy orange tree produces oranges, so a Christian being continually filled with the Spirit bears the fruit of the Spirit.[13]

An orange tree does not need to think about the fruit it will produce. It bears fruit because that is what it *naturally* does when it is well rooted and nourished.

What I want to draw out here is not how we can bear good fruit instead of bad.

The point is for us to throw our energy and effort into rooting ourselves deeply into God's love, trusting that His Spirit will bear good fruit through us as we do this.

As I've just said, the primary aim of the Spirit is to root us ever deeper within God's love.

Every fruit of the Spirit speaks of, and furthers, this primary aim of the Spirit.

So self-control, a product of the Spirit, is part of the Spirit's work to lead us further into the love of Jesus.

I had previously thought the main point of self-control was to help me avoid making poor decisions, but actually self-control is more about enabling me to consistently choose Jesus.

The difference, albeit subtle, is incredibly important.

(cont. from last page) filled with the Spirit, as he does in *Ephesians 5.18*, it carries a present continuous meaning. Paul is not encouraging us to be filled once with the Spirit, he is encouraging us to be filled 'continually' with the Spirit.

13. Credit to *Jon Tyrell* for that line.

The work of the Holy Spirit, God Himself, focuses on drawi
into Himself, not drawing us away from evil.

Of course, being drawn into God also draws us away from evil, but the focus is different!

We can walk away from evil without pushing into God, but we cannot push into God without walking away from evil.

The aim of self-control is to help us to pursue God, not to avoid sin!

The result of pursuing God?

Fleeing sin.

You could even say that when we sin, it is just because we slowed our pursuit of Jesus; we lost sight of Him and His love.

When we remain in the love of God we are living by faith, and continually living in faith leads us away from sin.

Just like Jesus.

He lived in continual agreement with God, full of love for God and so lived by faith.

The result?

He was sinless.

Sinlessness is a fruit of faithfulness.

Being sinless wasn't the focus of Jesus' life; being faithful to God was.[14]

---

14. And, as we've said before, He wanted to be faithful to God because He loved God.

If you want to get rid of darkness, don't push against the shadow.

Find a way to have more light.

Walking In The Light

The reason that many of us find ourselves overwhelmed with our own shortcomings, is because we mistakenly take responsibility for our transformation into our own hands.

When we believe this, we spend our effort focussing on all that needs correcting within us because we think it is our job to change ourselves.

We might as well attempt heart surgery on ourselves.

Not recommended.

Ultimately, we must place the responsibility for our growth and transformation squarely into the hands of Jesus.

Our hearts cannot be transformed by anyone other than God Himself.

We may be able to manufacture an illusion of change within us through controlling our behaviour, but only God can actually change the very fabric of who we are.

In order to be peaceful with the fact that our transformation is not in our own hands, we must understand that, through Jesus, God has already made us holy. He has clothed us in the purest of garments and invited us to approach Him at any moment of any day.[15]

We are not attempting to become holy through acting in a correct way, we are allowing the holiness that God has clothed us in to shape and

---

15. *Isaiah 1.18 & Hebrews 10.20.*

transform our behaviour.

We do not gain this holiness by our own merit; it is given by the graciousness of Christ.[16] Through His willing sacrifice He earned the right to call others to share and partake in His holiness and purity.

Somehow we have allowed ourselves to read in Scripture that Jesus' blood has made us holy, yet believed and professed that we are not holy.

When God says holy, He means holy.

We are now a holy, blameless and spotless people.[17]

Of course, it is a great mystery that we are holy yet still being transformed; free, yet continually being liberated. This is because holiness and freedom are not static states.

They are ever-unfolding realities.

Paul refers to this when he speaks of being transformed from glory to glory in *2 Corinthians 3.18*. We are already glorious, thanks to Jesus, at the same time as continually experiencing an ever-unfolding glory.

We can be confident before God because Jesus has clothed us irrevocably with His righteousness and invited us to walk boldly before the throne of the Father.[18]

Grace is our invitation and our justification for being in God's presence, and we are justified by grace in our best moments, and in our worst.

---

16. *Hebrews 10.14.*
17. *Isaiah 1.18 & 1 Peter 2.9.*
18. *Hebrews 4.16.*

We are justified by grace in *every* moment.[19]

Nothing can change that.

If we believe we are not good enough to be before God and be used by Him, we will either try to rush sorting ourselves out, or we will become despondent because of our inability to change ourselves.

Neither is true freedom.

If we truly long to live into the holiness and freedom given to us thanks to the Holy Spirit, then the solution is not our own effort.

The solution is Jesus.

Yes we have a responsibility to bring ourselves before Him, not passively waiting for Him to work within us, but proactively seeking Him and giving Him access to our hearts, minds and lives; and yes we can choose whether we make good decisions based on faith in Jesus, or not.

But ultimately, it is only Jesus who can actually *change* us.

We must fill our gaze with Him.

As we take our hands off the controls and allow Christ to lead us in our transformation, we find that He doesn't always do things as we would.

Often, He changes us in stages.

Explaining a layer at a time, unpicking miss-beliefs like an expert weaver un-picking a mistake.

God intends to make lasting changes.

---

[19]. *Romans 3.24 & Titus 3.7.*

This means re-calibrating us at every level. We may only see a surface issue, but God will un-pick us to our very core.

Are we willing to be changed at the centre of who we are?

For God to alter the very things we desire and the way we work?

Often Jesus works on parts of us that we aren't expecting Him to, at times faster than we would like, and at others far slower than we would desire. But the joy is this; as we put our freedom into His hands, we can be assured that He is unfolding His perfection within us in the perfect way.

So let us not hide when we are presented by our own shortcomings.

Let us not become despondent and ashamed.

Let us lift our chins and fill ourselves with the light of Jesus so that He can move within us, ever unfolding His perfection.

I Don't Know You

In the next chapter I want to further explore the topic of purity. How do we actually live in line with the blameless, pure people God has transformed us into by His grace?

What even *is* purity?

But before we move on, there are a couple of things I want to throw into the mix on this topic of sin.

Earlier I said that there are some actions that will never come from a place of faith.

It is also possible for an action that appears to be 'good', to in fact be sinful, because it isn't originating from faith.

Perhaps that is why Jesus said that some people would come to Him, telling Him that they'd prophesied in His name, but that His response would be to tell them to get away from Him, saying:

"I don't know you."[20]

Even though these people were prophesying, they did not *know* Jesus in their hearts. That meant that what they were doing wasn't originating from faith.

When we do something just because we think we 'ought' to, or because it is the 'right' thing to do, it may be worth just checking with the Holy Spirit to see if He is leading us in that moment.

Let's take a minute to ask the Spirit whether what we are doing is the best thing to be doing in that moment.

He may place a strong impression on us that it is, or that it isn't.

No matter how 'good' and 'godly' something appears, if the Spirit suggests that it isn't right for now, let us follow His lead.

How often do we maintain a set of actions because it is just 'what Christians do', without seeking God as to whether it is what *He* is leading us to do in that moment?

I'm not suggesting we question every rhythm or discipline of faith we have, or that we become unsure of doing anything because we haven't heard God specifically endorsing it, but let's ask ourselves whether we do what we do in our walk of faith because of a deep desire to know and follow the living Jesus, or whether we are doing it because it is what we've always done, and what we've been taught to do.

God has given us all authority on heaven and on earth, but He still

---

20. *Matthew 7.22-23.*

wants us to use it *with* Him, following *His* lead!

Now, let us not forget God's heart in this.

God wants to unveil an inordinate amount of His power on this earth. We can expect to do miracles, see resurrections and healings through us, by God's power.

But the point I'm trying to make is that as we evaluate our lives to see whether there is any 'sin' present, we must prioritise evaluating our hearts, not our actions, because even the best looking action could be coming from an un-whole motive.

Do you know and understand your own heart?

As the Holy Spirit helps you to look at yourself, let Him guide you to look through your actions, to see your heart.

Seek to be filled continually with the Holy Spirit and allow Him to undo your heart and put it back together.

Fill yourself with Jesus and trust *Him* for your holiness.

Do not just seek to imitate the *works* of Christ.

Imitate Christ Himself.

Two Little Asides

1. Making Confident Decisions

It would be incredibly easy at this point to become paralysed through a fear of making a decision that doesn't originate from a place of faith.

We can become so fearful of doing the wrong thing that we never make decisions, or we think that no decision is good enough to have truly originated from faith.

Let's remind ourselves of a couple of things.

God is for us.

He also doesn't always tell us every single thing that we are to do.

He doesn't always tell us what to wear, or what to eat that day.

He tells us enough for us to move forward, then things just seem to slot into place. Or sometimes that which was once cloudy, suddenly becomes clear.

God wants you to make brilliant decisions and choices.

If you can't hear Him on a decision, then make the best decision you can, prayerfully searching the Scriptures and taking counsel from mature Christian friends for wisdom. If you end up considering a decision that God is not for, He will let you know. If you are seeking Him with a soft heart, He isn't going to let you lead yourself down a dark path.

Think of Mary and Joseph.

Mary tells Joseph that she is pregnant before they're married and have slept together.

He wasn't expecting that.

He needs to go away to think about it:

> *Her husband Joseph, being a just man and unwilling to put her to shame, resolved to divorce her quietly.*
> MATTHEW 1.19 ESV

Joseph needs to make a tough decision and he hasn't heard God's

direction on it yet. Scripture tells us that he was a j
man; a man who had a good heart. He decides to divor
because that is what he thinks is the most just decis
circumstances:

> *But as he considered these things, behold, an angel of the LORD appeared to him in a dream, saying, "Joseph, son of David, do not fear to take Mary as your wife, for that which is conceived in her is from the Holy Spirit."*
> MATTHEW 1.20 ESV

Isn't it fascinating that God waited for Joseph to make a decision in his heart before He intervened and corrected it?

Sometimes when we are making a big decision, God seems silent.

But that doesn't mean we can't make a decision.

If we can't hear God, then we can make a decision based on who we know Him to be, and trust that if it isn't the correct decision He will let us know!

And if we make the decision that God desires us to make in the first place, then He doesn't need to break in and change our mind.

Silence isn't always a bad thing.

And then sometimes, we just have a choice.

Remember, the will of God is sometimes a land to explore and sometimes a path to stick to.

The key to making good decisions is having a soft heart and a clean ear.

If we are constantly living a life of love for Jesus, where we are attentive to what He may be saying and confident of His desire for goodness in

...ives, I believe we will work out how to live lives of faith, making consistently fantastic decisions.

2. Mistakes Happen

We sometimes make mistakes and poor decisions.

It happens when learning.

But God is exceptionally graceful.

Even when we make a mistake, if our heart is to love God and to live for Him, He will bring us back, teach us, refine us and set us again on our unique path of life with Him.

Think of King David—He committed adultery and murder.

But David's heart was for God—he was a man after God's own heart.[21]

Even though David made a few really bad decisions, underneath it all he still loved God. And God, because He knew David's heart, set people around him who could correct him.

David repented and moved forward.

Sometimes we can be so fearful of making a mistake, or feel so guilty because of something we have done, that we forget God is good and that Jesus paid for sin so that we can learn from our mistakes, rather than die because of them.

Good news.

Nothing should make us fearful of God anymore.

---

21. *1 Samuel 13.14.*

Not even our own mistakes.

Looking On

As we come to the end of this chapter let us reflect on the opportunity that lies before us.

Jesus has corrected the misunderstanding that sin is all about the outside, when in fact it is all about the inside.

Sin starts as a lack of faith in Jesus in our hearts, that then works its way out to our words and works.

But in the same way, the righteousness that Jesus offers us through His blood and by His grace, can set up home in our hearts and work its way out to heavenly behaviour and actions.

Jesus longs for us to lean all our lives upon Him, putting our faith in Him in all we do.

In doing so, His Spirit will set to work within our hearts, minds and lives, bearing good fruit through us as He roots us in the love of the Father.

This life of faith in Jesus will lead us into God's heart and purposes, and draw us away from all darkness and evil.

So let us continually remind ourselves of the way of life that Jesus demonstrated and holds out to us to experience for ourselves, through living by faith in Him, empowered by the Spirit, and enthralled by God's love.

5. FIRE ISN'T THE ABSENCE OF WATER

What purity is,

not what it isn't.

The Process

Having talked about sin in the last chapter, it's logical to talk about purity in this chapter, as purity and sin are so closely linked.

However, before we start talking about purity, I want to take a moment to reflect on the journey so far.

I hope that in reading the past few chapters you've been able to follow some of the processes that I've been through in my life.

I have grown to understand that everything God has placed within me is designed to come to fruition as I lean fully upon Him. The Spirit has taught me that the best way for me to live this life of total dependency is to choose it from a deep love for Jesus, and that this deep love comes as a response to seeing Him and encountering His love and affection for me.

Whenever we see Him, we see His love, and whenever we see His love, our love for Him grows.

With this new centre to my life, I came to a new understanding about what pleases God and what doesn't.

In *Turning Sin Outside In*, I explained that sin isn't fundamentally about me doing something against the 'rules'. Sin is when I am not depending upon Jesus.

Having a moment when I am not remaining in Him.

And as we saw in the chapter, *The Good News That Keeps Getting Better*, being 'in' God is about remaining in God's love, abiding in it and allowing all that we do to flow from that place.

Our callings will happen and flourish around us if we remain, if we stay, in Him.

And if all we do flows from being in Him, living by the Spirit, then sin will arise less and less in our lives as a result:

> *But I say, walk by the Spirit, and you will not gratify the desires of the flesh.*
> GALATIANS 5.16 ESV

We know that sin can be defeated in this way because it is how Jesus remained sinless.

It's another aspect of the complex simplicity of following Christ. Instead of trying to achieve a lifestyle based on 'not doing the wrong things'—a very complicated and defensive way of living—Jesus invites us to simply follow Him, the man who fulfilled the entire old covenant law[1] by following the lead of His Father in heaven.

It is the simple call to follow Jesus, yet the wonder of the impact that following Him has upon us.

With this process in mind, let us look at the topic of purity.

In light of all that has been said in previous chapters, how can we recalibrate our understanding of purity?

Purity

For many Christians the subject of 'purity' seems to be an incredibly hot topic. We are inundated with thoughts and teaching on what is, and what isn't, 'pure'.

As I considered purity in my own life, I realised that, in light of everything God had been teaching me, purity could not simply be about 'doing the right things', and abstaining from 'doing wrong'.

---

1. *Matthew 5.17.*

If something is pure it means it is uncontaminated.

It means that it contains only one thing.

For example, pure iron contains only iron. Nothing but good old 'Fe'.

When we talk about purity in the Christian context, we are very good at naming what impurities must be absent in order for something to be pure.

We have a whole long list of what isn't pure.

But if you talked to a metal expert and asked them to explain what pure iron is, I doubt that they would describe it by listing the impurities that aren't present.

That would take a seriously long time.

Instead, I imagine they would tell you it is iron that is uncontaminated by anything else.

They would define it by what it is, not what it isn't.

Fire isn't the absence of water, it is the presence of fire.

And so it is with Christian purity.

If purity is not defined by what it isn't, then what is it defined by?

What would the one thing present in Christian purity be?

Purity Isn't Just The Absence Of Sin

As I reflected on purity, I realised that I had spent a great deal of time trying to motivate my faith by fighting against what I was doing wrong.

I wanted to be so cleansed from all evil and 'sin' that it became the aim of my faith. My ultimate objective was to not make any mistakes.

There are numerous problems with this way of thinking.

You see, when we make overcoming sin the object of our faith, we are missing the very key to living into the sinlessness Jesus has gifted us by His grace, and modelled in His life.

When I say that God Himself is the objective of faith, I have no doubt that you will agree. But if I'm honest with you, I'm not sure that I really understood what it meant for God to be the object of my faith for quite a long time.

When I looked at how I used to live and what filled my mind most, it was not God. My life and my mind were filled most with my attempts to do right and avoid doing what was wrong in an effort to please God, and to live up to what I perceived to be His standards.

I wonder what each of us would find if we looked at ourselves honestly and asked the question:

"What is the object of my faith?"

For as noble as focussing on 'doing the right things' is, it wasn't Jesus' primary focus, and so it need not be ours.

A Bored Free Person

We know that our old self was crucified with him in order that the body of sin might be brought to nothing, so that we would no longer be enslaved to sin.

For one who has died has been set free from sin.
ROMANS 6.6-7 ESV

If the aim of our faith is only to be free from 'sin', what happens when we are?

When Jesus returns all sin and evil will be eternally destroyed and will have no part in the new creation.

If we think that our greatest emotion when Jesus returns will be a relief that our war with sin is finally over and that we are finally free, we have sorely missed the point.

Jesus has already freed us from sin and made us holy.

He has unbound our hands and parted our lips. If our reaction to the return of Jesus is relief that we can finally be free from sin, I wonder if He will turn to us and say:

"You've been free from that for a while."

Having 'getting free from sin' as our primary goal in life is like a convict released from prison pledging to continue trying to break out of his cell; it's already been opened for him!

Believe me, I understand how easy it is to feel like we are still bound by sin. Our mistakes do affect us and pull us and others down. I'm not denying that.

But what I am trying to say is that the aim of the Christian faith cannot be to achieve the righteousness, freedom and holiness that Jesus, by His blood and grace, has already clothed us in.

Being a believer is not about trying to obtain a new identity through correct behaviour; it is about allowing the Holy Spirit to reshape our behaviour to the new identity we have been gifted by God.

So if we are already liberated from sin, then what is our purpose?

Being Free For God

In the previous chapter we saw that Scripture teaches that Jesus lived a perfect, pure and sinless life.

He was perfect, not because He pursued sinlessness, but because He pursued faithfulness to God, and His faithfulness to God was a result of His love of God.

We are invited to live just as He did[2], not focusing on being free from sin, but focusing on being free *for* God.

God has set us free so that we can know Him, live with Him, experience Him and be in fellowship with Him. *He* is the object of our faith![3]

Paul got this. The goal of his life became knowing God, knowing Jesus.

This is what he says in *Philippians*:

> *[For my determined purpose is] that I may know Him [that I may progressively become more deeply and intimately acquainted with Him, perceiving and recognising and understanding the wonders of His person more strongly and more clearly], and that I may in that same way, come to know the power overflowing from His resurrection [which it exerts over believers].*
> PHILIPPIANS 3.10 AMP

Now I know there's a lot to grasp there, so it's worth reading a couple of times to understand more fully.

In the passage, Paul is saying two things. Firstly, he explains what his life purpose is, and secondly, he explains what effect pursuing that life purpose will have on him.

---

2. *1 John 2.6.*

3. He happens to be the author and perfecter of it too.

His life purpose is to get to know Jesus more and more, to gradually see more of God and to grow in relationship with Him.

In other words, to be a true seeker of God.

He lived to know God and to be known by Him.

He goes on to say, *"And that I may in that same way, come to know the power overflowing from His resurrection."*[4]

For me, this is the really exciting part because the words *"in that same way"* are pivotal.

Paul says that he can experience the power of the resurrection of Jesus in his life, by living to know God more and more.

Paul is telling his readers in Philippi that the pursuit of knowing God leads to experiencing the fullness of the power of God in our lives and around us.

The list of things that the power of the resurrection of Jesus has left open and possible for us is long and amazing. And one of them is freedom from sin.

The by-product of growing in our relationship with Jesus is an ever-unfolding freedom.

Paul, in the space of just a verse, paints a picture of immense possibility and hope.

He not only clearly articulates his single life purpose, but also highlights what that purpose can lead to for any follower of Jesus; a complete freedom available through knowing the living God in ever-increasing measure.

---

[4] *Philippians 3.10b AMP.*

Too Good To Miss

If we, like Paul, live growing in the knowledge of Jesus, we will come to see more of God's character.

God wants to show us all of His goodness, and all the good gifts He has for us.[5] And when we see anything that He has for us, we will *want* to let go of anything that is not from God so that we can live into all that God has for us.

Sometimes letting go of an insecurity or stronghold is incredibly challenging and daunting because we have learnt to use them for protection and safety.

Yet if we allow God to reveal all that He has in store for us, we will gladly let go of any other thing in our grasp in the sheer excitement of laying hold of that which God is offering.

It's like walking up to a fresh fruit stall with your arms full of mouldy bananas.

When you see all the fresh fruit available, you drop the mouldy bananas because you've seen something far better for you, something you want more.

But the even more wonderful truth is that we don't have to do this alone.

Through showing us God's kindness, the Spirit inspires and enables us to let go of anything that isn't from God in order grasp all that God has for us:

---

5. Good gifts, not in the sense of a father spoiling their child by giving them everything the child asks for irrespective of whether it be good or bad for the them, but good gifts that a perfect Father knows are good for his children!

> *Do you presume on the riches of his kindness and forb
> and patience, not knowing that God's kindness is 1
> lead you to repentance?*
> ROMANS 2.4 ESV

The best reason for repentance is not regret.[6]

The best reason for repentance is seeing God's kindness.[7]

Seeing that there is more available.

That there is a higher way of life, a way of life we want to live more than the one we have been living.

Fresh fruit is on offer instead of mouldy bananas.

At times we will feel deeply convicted of a mistake or poor decision we've made, and we will want to repent of our mistake.

However, let us not just repent to be free from our mistakes, let us repent in response to all that Jesus offers!

Let us repent in response to *Him*.

When the Spirit puts His finger on something He wants to change within us, it is not because He is angry at our errors; He is urging us to see all the goodness that is possible for us through Him.

The conviction of the Spirit is an invitation, not a guilt trip.

Trying to motivate ourselves to let go of something is much harder than wanting to let go of what is in our hands because we've seen something better.

---

6. *2 Corinthians 7.10.*

7. *Romans 2.4.*

Fire Isn't The Absence Of Water

God is setting you free *for* things, not just *from* things.

His kindness, not your regret, is intended to lead you to repentance.

Not That I've Already Attained This...

Not that I have attained [this ideal], or have been made perfect, but I press on to lay hold of and make my own that for which Christ has laid hold of me and made his own.

I do not consider, brethren, that I have captured and made it my own [yet]; but one thing I do [it is my aspiration]: forgetting what lies behind and straining for what lies ahead,

I press on toward the goal to win the [supreme and heavenly] prize to which God in Christ Jesus is calling us upward.
PHILIPPIANS 3.12-14 AMP

Just after he has laid out what he believes to be possible in *Philippians 3.10*, Paul assures the readers of his letter that he doesn't think he has reached perfection in his life yet.

He still has moments where faith isn't what he chooses.

Don't we all!

But Paul also wants his readers to see that he is looking forwards, not backwards.

Paul wanted his eyes to be filled with what is possible through Jesus, not with the mistakes he had already made, recently or historically.

Paul knew that the way to become like Jesus was by beholding Jesus. If we spend all of our time considering our mistakes and shortcomings, we begin to think they are the most pressing things in our lives.

They don't have to be.

If you want to move beyond living your Christian life as a mere sin-management programme, do what Paul did; look forward to what is possible through the saving grace of Christ Jesus.

Ask the Holy Spirit to enable you to put regrets in their proper place: behind you.

Fill your eyes and mind with God Himself.

> *Set your minds on things that are above, not on things that are on earth.*
>
> *For you have died, and your life is hidden with Christ in God.*
> COLOSSIANS 3.2-3 ESV

Christ did not lay hold of you so that you would continually be living a life consumed by your own shortcomings.

He laid hold of you to be with Him for all eternity and to be transformed by His Spirit today—right now

If Jesus wanted you to wait until He returns to experience the power overflowing from His resurrection, He needn't have sent His Holy Spirit prior to His return.

But He did send His Holy Spirit.

And that means that there is sanctification happening right now. His perfection is unfolding within you as you live on earth:

> *And we all, with unveiled face, beholding the glory of the Lord, are being transformed into the same image from one degree of glory to another.*
> 2 CORINTHIANS 3.18A ESV

So what do you want to focus on?

Your mistakes?

Or the perfection of Jesus that is unfolding within you, here and now, through the Holy Spirit?

Focussing on what lies ahead and not what is behind, does not mean we pretend we don't make mistakes.

Quite the opposite.

In spite of our mistakes we look to Jesus.

So humbled by the grace of God, we pick ourselves up and continue to behold and pursue Christ with everything we are, because that is the least that the grace of God demands and deserves.

He demands it not by ultimatum, but by presenting us with such delightful possibilities that all we want to do is choose them.

The way to live into the purity that Christ has won for us is simple and single.

Focus on getting to know Him more:

> *[For my determined purpose is] that I may know Him [that I may progressively become more deeply and intimately acquainted with Him, perceiving and recognizing and understanding the wonders of His person more strongly and more clearly].*
> PHILIPPIANS 3.10 AMP

Through growing in our deep acquaintance with Jesus, we will see the power of the resurrection of Jesus overflow into our lives.

The power that makes us just like Him.

The door stands open for us to become freer than we've ever known, or even dared think possible.

I do not want to limit what Jesus can do in my life.

It is far too exciting to miss.

Single-Mindedness

One thing I have asked of the Lord, that will I seek, inquire of and [insistently] require: that I may dwell in the house of the Lord [in His presence] all the days of my life, to behold and gaze upon the beauty [the sweet attractiveness and the delightful loveliness] of the Lord and to meditate, consider, and inquire in His temple.
PSALM 27.4 AMP

Purity is the single-minded pursuit of the person of Jesus.

Not because you have to, not because you ought to, but because it has become your greatest desire to.

Paul had this single-minded focus, as we saw in *Philippians 3*, and King David writes with a similar sentiment in *Psalm 27*.

David asks God for one thing.

One single thing:

To be with God all the days of his life, gazing on the beauty of God, getting to know God more.

This is true purity.

As you consider yourself and whether you are living a pure life, don't ask whether you are abstaining from the wrong things and practicing the correct ones.

Ask yourself how passionate you are about the person of Jesus.

Not just what He has done or does, or what He could do through you, but Jesus Himself.

Ask yourself whether you're growing in love for the person of Jesus, not just His miracles or even the wonders of what He says.

Just Him.

I firmly believe that the people who have a single-minded desire to progressively know Jesus more and more will naturally lead lives that grow in reflecting the lifestyle of Jesus.

Their passions will reflect His passions, their words will reflect His words and their actions will reflect His actions.

I strongly recommend that we all re-evaluate our self-assessments of our purity, the measuring sticks of our holiness and the plumb lines of how sinful we think we are or are not.

I urge us to trust that the heart that God created within us will *want* to let go of anything not of Him as we see the kindness, goodness and loveliness of Christ.

If we are to be people of true purity, then our sole passion must be Jesus, and our purpose needs to be to behold Him, progressively growing in knowledge of His marvellous character.

A Closing Note

Throughout the last few chapters I have often talked about us 'knowing God', or 'loving God', as being the most important thing for us to focus on in our lives.

These phrases can seem vague and impractical.

I do not mean to be impractical with my words, but I feel strongly that we each need to learn how we love God as only we can. What it looks like for each of us, as unique people made in God's image, to live for Him.

I am hesitant to put forward specific practises and disciplines because I do not want to rob us of the opportunity to hear the Holy Spirit lead us into how we are each designed to live with, and love, God.

There is no doubt that the Holy Spirit will lead us all directly into Scripture because Scripture is full to bursting with God's heart and voice for all humankind, and Scripture is the scales upon which every revelation is to be weighed.

And granted, the Holy Spirit often inspires us through the practice and lifestyles of others. Just as Paul encouraged people to imitate Him imitating Jesus[8], I am inspired by the lives of others who are following Jesus.

However, we must be careful to see that it is actually the Holy Spirit using another's life to inspire us, as opposed to us assuming that another person's lifestyle is the one correct way of living.

We only imitate others because the Holy Spirit uses them to help us to work out our own unique ways of imitating Jesus.

No one person, other than Jesus, has the way, because Jesus Christ Himself is the Way.

I believe that God is asking us tough questions about ourselves. He is certainly asking them of me.

---

8. *1 Corinthians 11.1.*

We have a chance to let go of any conceited motivations that may be hidden in our hearts of why we follow Jesus.

We have an invitation to be refocused and restored to the blissful simplicity of the Christian life.

We get to be with God, to know Him, and to be known by Him now and for all eternity.

He is wonderful enough to continually and forever capture our attention, and to inspire us.

We need no greater motivation in our lives than God Himself.

He is the source of every good thing.

As we close this chapter, I pray that we all may be cut back by the Holy Spirit, again and again, to the wonderful simplicity of living pure lives; that we may live with the single purpose of becoming progressively acquainted with the wonders of the persons of God, more and more.

And, in that same way, we will see our lives changed by the power of the resurrection of Jesus, liberating us from anything and everything that could stand in the way of God's love for us, and our reciprocating love for Him.

What truly good news!

6. PERMISSION OR BLESSING?

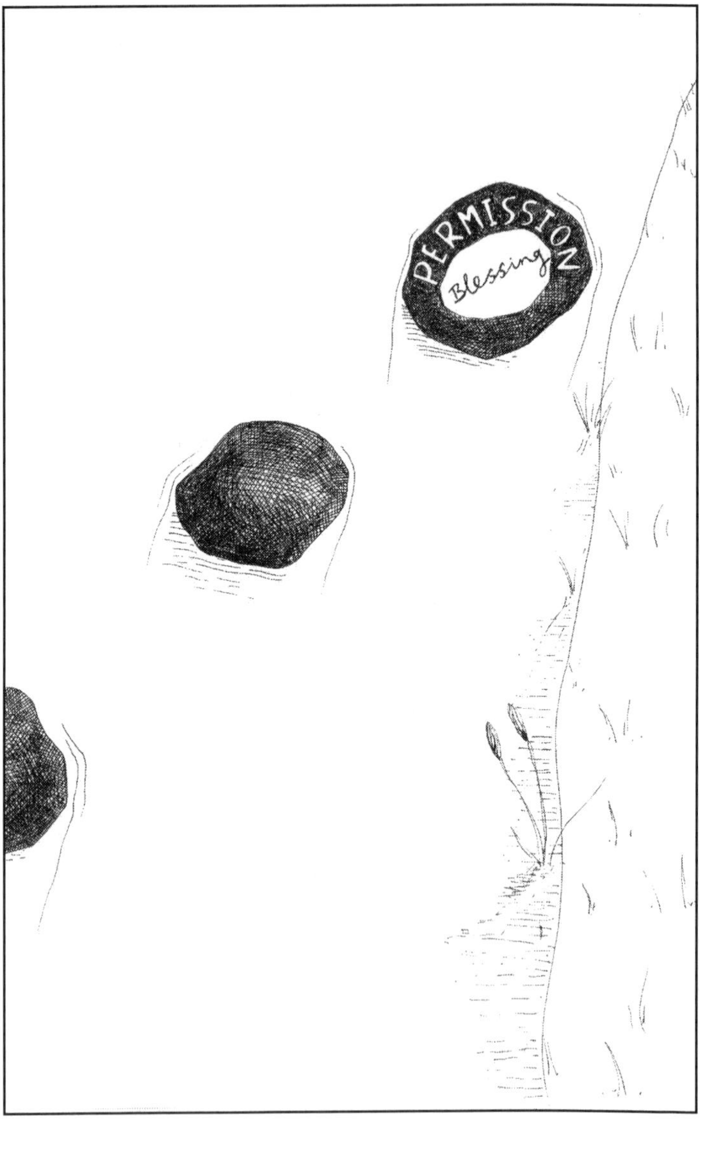
PERMISSION
Blessing

The Problem

When Rebekah and I started going out, it was a really exciting time in my life. God was doing a lot in me, shaping and teaching me.

By bringing out insecurities, fears and misguided beliefs, God had been explaining how He could change the parts of me that weren't whole.

He had been setting me free at the very core of my being, changing my desires.

The past five chapters have all come from reflecting on this time in my life. God had been turning some of my beliefs of what Christianity was about upside-down and outside-in.

As Rebekah and I began our relationship, I realised that I was poorly equipped to pursue a relationship in light of all God had been teaching me.

You see, my understanding of a godly pre-marriage relationship had been all about 'healthy boundaries' and ensuring that we maintained spiritual, emotional and physical 'purity'.

I had thought that we needed to set up boundaries to ensure that we didn't overstep the mark. I thought it was all about not going 'too far'.

Now, it is easy to think that I'm trying to refer none too subtly to the physical elements of a relationship, but that is only part of it.

Think about it emotionally. How much are you allowed to tell each other and rely on each other? How much do you hold back until you're married?

Spiritually, are we allowed to pray together? Are we allowed to spend time worshipping together? What about sharing revelations and Scriptures that excite our hearts?

What are the boundaries? How do I make sure we don't 'mess up'?

This is where I, and Rebekah and I, hit upon the problem.

God had been teaching me that sin doesn't originate with an action. Sin originates in my heart and is about whether I am living from a place of faith; a place of total dependence on Jesus.

Thanks to the revelations and works of God in my life, I saw that living for Jesus wasn't about trying to maintain a correct set of behaviours. This meant that the health of my relationship with Rebekah wasn't going to be measured by what we managed to abstain from and what we managed to practice.

Rebekah and I realised that we needed to work out a new understanding of what a healthy relationship looks like to Jesus, and in doing so, we discovered that there was another way of approaching our walk with Jesus altogether.

So much of the 'boundary' language is reserved, almost exclusively, for discussions around romantic relationships. But as Rebekah and I journeyed in it together, we realised that the revelations we received on this particular topic actually significantly impacted the rest of our faith as well.

Although some of this chapter will be viewed through the lens of mine and Rebekah's experience of going out, it is by no means limited to a romantic context. In fact, I believe it goes far, far beyond it, affecting the core of our walks with Jesus.

Two Sides

There are two sides of being a Christian.

Both are true and both are essential.

On the one hand we have been called to serve God, the King not just of this world, but of the entire cosmos.

By His grace we have been brought back into His household, no longer to serve ourselves, but Him.

If God only called us to serve Him as servants, without rights or claims to anything, requiring us to do whatever He commanded, it would be an act of extraordinary grace.

It would be entirely reasonable for God never to invite us beyond the status of servants.

We could serve Him for all eternity and never fulfil the debt we owe.

But the story of the prodigal son in *Luke 15* doesn't end with the Father accepting the younger son's plea to be a servant:

> *I will arise and go to my father, and I will say to him, 'Father, I have sinned against heaven and before you.*
>
> *I am no longer worthy to be called your son. Treat me as one of your hired servants.'*
>
> *And he arose and came to his father. But while he was still a long way off, his father saw him and felt compassion, and ran and embraced him and kissed him.*
>
> *And the son said to him, 'Father, I have sinned against heaven and before you. I am no longer worthy to be called your son.'*
>
> *But the father said to his servants, 'Bring quickly the best robe, and put it on him, and put a ring on his hand, and shoes on his feet.*
>
> *And bring the fattened calf and kill it, and let us eat and celebrate.*

> *For this my son was dead, and is alive again; he was lost, and is found.' And they began to celebrate.*
> LUKE 15.18-24 ESV

The son in the parable hopes that his father has enough mercy and grace to accept him as a servant.

But what a father!

Although his son has squandered his love, kindness and inheritance, the father runs to him and celebrates his return. He welcomes him, not only as a highly honoured guest, but also as a dearly loved member of the family.

As if he'd never sinned.

This is the other side of the coin; God has invited us to be far more than just servants.

Thanks to Jesus, He has brought us into His house as His children, as if we'd never sinned.

If we believe that God has welcomed us into His house as mere servants, then we underestimate His kindness and His grace.

Of course it is true that we can never afford to forget that God is King; that He rules and has all dominion and power. That is who He is.

But we must also respond to His invitation to be His children and His friends.

Just because our Father is the King, does not mean we stop relating to Him as His children and His friends.

Embarking on our new relationship, Rebekah and I realised that having a 'boundary' focussed relationship and faith actually came from a servant mindset.

If God has called us His children, how do we relate to our Father not just as servants, but also as friends?

Servants And Friends

I do not call you servants any longer, for the servant does not know what his master is doing. But I have called you my friends, because I have made known to you everything that I have heard from my Father."
JOHN 15.15 AMP

In *John 15*, Jesus elevates His disciples' perceived relationship with Him from being one of service to one of friendship.

It's like being befriended by a queen. Just because we are friends with the queen doesn't mean she stops being a queen; it just means she's also our friend. And to relate to her only as her subject, undermines her choice to have us as a friend.

There will of course be moments where it is still right to act as a subject to a friend who is the queen, but unless that is needed, our default can be that of a friend.

Some might say that *John 15.15* is an elevation offered to Jesus' 12 disciples alone, and that we today are to remain as servants.

The issue with this is that Jesus promises us His Holy Spirit, who will remind us of everything that Jesus taught.[1]

If Jesus taught His disciples that they are no longer just servants, but friends, then the Holy Spirit must be wanting to teach us the same lesson.

---

1. *John 14.26.*

Because the Spirit teaches us what Jesus taught His disciples.

There is an invitation extended to us to be friends of God!

Not because we deserve or have earned it.

But because God Himself desires it and has earned it on our behalf through the death of His Son.

We are faced with a choice.

Will we stay with the perception that we are only God's servants, or will we explore what it means to be His friends?

Back To The Problem

As Rebekah and I discussed our relationship, we realised that we wanted to work from a position of being God's friends, not just His servants.

In friendships, your primary motivation is to please your friends, not merely to obey them.

A friendship doesn't flourish if you only do what the other asks of you, if you only do the bare minimum.

Friends love to do what their friends love.

Servants ask their masters, *"What am I allowed to do?"*, whereas friends ask their friends, *"What do you love me doing?"*

Rebekah and I wanted to work out what God delighted over, not just what He allowed.

What does God bless, not just what does He permit?

This way of operating with God depends on the Holy Spirit speaking to us and making the things that please God pleasing to our hearts too.

Naturally, Rebekah and I learnt from those around us; we weren't interested in trying to re-invent the wheel! But we wanted to work out how God desired *us* to develop our relationship.

Because we are all unique people, there must be unique elements to our relationships that only God knows about.

Rebekah and I had four friends with whom we would talk and discuss what we felt the Holy Spirit was blessing for us. They helped us to discover what God desired for our relationship, but they weren't primarily concerned with making sure that Rebekah and I didn't cross any 'boundaries'; their primary concern was that we were wholly following the Spirit's lead.

During this process, Rebekah and I discovered a number of delightful things about operating this way with Jesus.

Firstly, we discovered that what God was blessing for us was different to what He was blessing for others around us.

We need to become peaceful with the idea that God blesses different things for different people at different times. Not just in relationships, but in every aspect of life.

It is important for us to be confident and satisfied with what God is blessing for us at any given moment. It is so easy to become jealous of the freedom that a fellow believer has been allowed by God.

But God gently calls us to be content with our own portions.

There may be moments where we abuse this understanding, this freedom to do as we discern what God is blessing. However, if we truly want to be friends with God, then we won't want to abuse His blessing.

If we find ourselves abusing God's blessing, trying to use it to legitimise doing whatever we want, we've lost sight of the point, and will have stepped outside of His blessing.

However, we need not create a list of 'do's' and 'don'ts' to try and stop ourselves and others from abusing God's blessing. If we do that, we will end up blocking people from discovering God's blessings for themselves, and limit people to living as servants, as opposed to friends.

The second thing that Rebekah and I learnt was that going after what God was blessing meant that we didn't go beyond what He permitted.

So often, if we are most mindful of what God does and doesn't permit, we stare continually at the boundary lines, rather than enjoying the area enclosed by the boundary lines.

We end up standing at the fence looking at what lies beyond, thinking it more pleasant than what lies within. We don't realise that, if we just turned around, there is a luscious green landscape waiting to be explored and enjoyed!

This is probably where we get our notions of 'boundaries' from.

Scripture tells us that there are certain things that God never blesses, so we then labelled those things as definitive 'boundary lines'.

They became the 'rules'.

And we began to believe that if we break the rules, we are sinning.

But this is only a half-truth!

The actions aren't sin because they're objectively wrong to do.

As we've already seen, they're sin because the choice to do them *cannot* have come from a place of faith in Jesus.

So what does this actually mean for us?

It means that we can live in the assurance that God w
something He doesn't permit.

Which in turn means that we don't need to create a list of what is permitted and what isn't.

If we live as people wanting to *please* God, rather than just *obey* Him, we won't cross boundaries because we won't want to do something that God doesn't take delight in us doing.

In *1 Corinthians* Paul tells his readers to:

> *Follow the way of love.*
> 1 CORINTHIANS 14.1A ESV

Love always leads us to good, not to evil.

If we are following the way of love, the way of a friend seeking to please their friend, we will find ourselves naturally walking away from any wrong.

This way of love is not a sentiment, or a good-willed feeling. It is a person—Jesus Christ.

And Jesus has a perfect understanding of what truly leads to abundant life, and what doesn't.

His blessings then flow from this understanding.

He blesses that which leads to life, and does not bless that which doesn't.

We must remember that Jesus is not restraining us by clearly outlining what He blesses; He is liberating us:

> *The [boundary] lines [of the land] have fallen for me in*
> *pleasant places;*
> *Indeed, my heritage is beautiful to me.*
> PSALM 16.6 AMP

The third thing that Rebekah and I learnt was that living focussed on what God was blessing helped us to move away from fear.

There were moments in our relationship where we suddenly felt the Holy Spirit tell us that we had done something that God wasn't blessing, such as relying on each other too much, or not enough.

In these moments, had the health of our relationship been defined by whether or not we 'crossed boundaries', it would have been all too easy for us to run from our mistakes and try to create more rules to ensure we never made them again.

But that wouldn't have solved the problem.

The root from which the action came would still be there, only buried under a set of rules.

Instead of running away in fear of our mistakes, Rebekah and I were able to look at ourselves and ask questions as to why we had over-relied on each other, or under-relied on each other. We got to see the root, the heart, and then allow God to correct us.

We mustn't, and needn't, live in fear.

Not even of doing the 'wrong' thing.

When the Holy Spirit convicts us, it is to change us, not to shame us.

Too often believers can be so determined not to step over the boundary lines, that they never understand why their hearts wanted to overstep the line in the first place.

If a heart that wants to rebel isn't changed, then it is not free.

Jesus made it possible to be free in our very hearts.

He can actually change what we *want* to do.

Would we rather never make a mistake, but be forever battling a heart that wants all kinds of untoward things, or would we like to run the risk of making a mistake, yet also open ourselves up to total transformation that can lead to our hearts actually wanting what God wants?

Beyond Romance

I have talked a number of times in previous chapters about not doing something because we are merely obliged to, but because it is our desire to.

I've written about this because I believe that the healthiest and most whole relationships involve our most passionate emotions as well as our best choices.

And our walk with Jesus need be no different.

God has hidden His kingdom within the hearts of humankind. That kingdom comes about through us as we agree with God. But agreement flows best from love, not obligation.[2]

Consider these two scriptures:

> *In all your ways know, recognise, and acknowledge Him and He will direct and make straight and plain your paths.*
> PROVERBS 3.5 AMP

---

2. Please do remind yourself of this in the subsection, *"The Power Of Agreement"*, in chapter 3.

> *Delight yourself also in the Lord, and He will give you the desires and secret petitions of your heart*
> PSALM 37.4 AMP

Can you see the subtle difference between the two?

In *Proverbs 3* the writer is calling us to acknowledge God in all we do; to take the time to see His hand at work in our lives, and to tell Him that we see His involvement.

The outcome of doing this is a straightforward life. *Proverbs 3* promises that God will give those who acknowledge Him a clear and direct path.

The difference in *Psalm 37* is the word *"delight"*.

Servants acknowledge their masters, but friends delight in their friends.

I'm not suggesting that *Proverbs 3* is flawed; it is stunning advice that we get to build our lives upon.

But if we settle for *just* acknowledging God, we miss out on the assurance of *Psalm 37*.

You see, the promised outcome of being someone who is delighted by God, is that the desires, yearnings and wants of their heart happen.

The things they long for and dream of, begin to come to pass.

I'm not saying that any wanton desire we may have will come to pass if we delight in God.

The result that delighting in God has on our hearts is a total refinement and transformation of their desires.

As we delight in Him, moved by His love for us, it changes us and changes what we want.

Our hearts are meant to be filled with God-given desires.

As He changes us and turns our hearts from stone to flesh, those heavenly desires begin to beat within.

If we hold onto the belief that we are to relate to God merely as servants, we are only seeing the beginning of the story. An essential start, but only the beginning!

Operating just as servants of God will result in us being people who acknowledge God, but do not truly delight in Him.

Acknowledging Him is good, but there is far more for us than that.

To truly experience the joy of seeing all of our God-given desires fulfilled, we must lose ourselves in love for Him.

In order to be people who dare to be moved by love over obligation, we must know that God has called us to be friends. He has promoted us!

All by His good grace.

There lies before us an invitation from God to engage with Him as friends; an opportunity to live asking God what He blesses, not just what He permits.

As we each reflect on our relationship with God, will we dare to truly accept His grace and become His friends?

Will we allow our place of friendship with Him to affect all of our decisions, mindsets and perceptions?

Will we ask God what He allows, or will we ask Him what He wants?

What He permits, or what He blesses?

The Need For Good Ears

To relate to God as friends, focussing on what He's blessing not just what He permits, requires us to be able to hear His voice and to respond to His lead.

We need to be sensitive to His promptings because otherwise we will not know what He is blessing for us, and we may not sense if His blessings change.

If we don't believe and trust that the Holy Spirit speaks to us and guides us, or if we don't value God's voice and presence highly, then we will find it hard to operate as His friends.

Often we Christians have shied away from talking about what God is blessing for individuals, or groups, because of the potential for the teaching to be abused; for people to pretend that they have heard God blessing them doing very un-Christ-like things.

But just because a truth can be abused does not mean it should be ignored.

For example, in *Matthew 5.17* Jesus tells His disciples that He hasn't come to do away with the old covenant law, but to fulfil it.

This law had been mis-taught and distorted for many years by the Pharisees. They used it to control, manipulate and cripple God's people.

But does Jesus say that He is going to do away with the law?

Absolutely not.

The law in itself was good and perfect, but it was twisted by humans for their own purposes.

Something similar has happened in the whole area of hearing the

Spirit speak to us and direct us; people have used this truth as a means to their own end and it has resulted in lots of pain and confusion.

Yet the remedy is not to do away with the truth that the Holy Spirit speaks to us.

The remedy is to cling to it more strongly than ever, teaching the truth faithfully, and choosing to live it out with integrity.

People will not get away with abusing God's truth. They will answer to Him. The only thing within our control here and now is whether we each choose to live into the truths that God reveals to us in the Scriptures, by His Spirit.

Each of us is responsible for ourselves, our faith and our walk with the Lord.

So, regardless of those around us and regardless of fear, we have the choice to respond to God's invitation of friendship, or not.

We can choose to stay 'safer' inside the boundaries of servant-hood, but if we do, we will not experience true freedom and joy found in friendship with God.

Instead of self-evaluating how we perceive ourselves to be doing, putting our confidence in our ability to adhere to a set of standards, we get to turn to the Father and ask Him;

"What do you want for me right now?" and, *"What do you delight in me doing?"*

His response may be the same as before, or it may have changed.

That's up to Him in His wisdom.

Are we ready to respond to God revealing His desires for us, open handed enough to surrender when He changes His blessing, and t enough to walk in the fullness of His blessing?

Are we willing to accept God's graceful invitation to be His friends?

The Completed Circle

True delight in God is only found through accepting His promotion to friendship with Him. That friendship means that we become increasingly motivated by a deep love for God, because friends love their friends.

We cannot manufacture this love.

Yet again, we arrive at the same point we have in previous chapters; in order to grow in love for God, we must see and experience God's love for us, His friends.

To experience more of His love and affection, we need to be with Him, we must enjoy the presence of God, allowing Him to speak to us.

We must be seekers of God.

Those who seek, find; those who find must carefully mind what they find, and then hold onto it, keeping it safe.

To believe in what God reveals to us, we need faith, a gift from God.

Living from this faith, this gift, leads us in the way of love, which is the person of Jesus; and constantly living from that place of having faith in Him takes us in the opposite direction to the way of sin.

This pursuit of Jesus Christ, untainted by anything else, is purity.

For purity is not the absence of impurity, it is the presence of one single thing—a growing, fierce passion for Jesus.

And in following Jesus, we discover how exceedingly gracious and loving He is, as He calls us to be His friends, not just His servants.

7. RESETTING DEFAULT SETTINGS

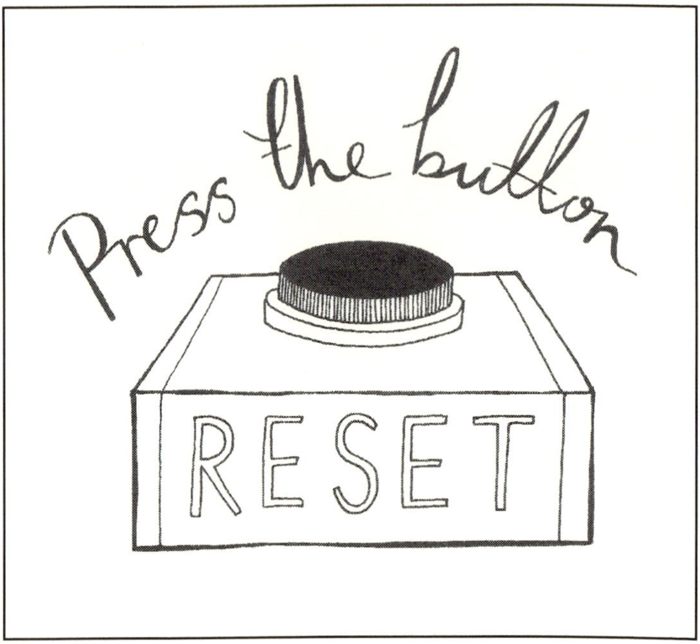
Press the button
RESET

The Place From Which We Live

As followers of Jesus, absolutely everything we do and encounter in life can be reconsidered in light of the victory of Jesus, and this includes how we perceive ourselves.

We get to regard ourselves anew, because the moment we come to faith in Jesus we undergo a re-birth.[1]

This re-birth changes our nature; we become different people.

By God's grace we go from being a sinner to being a saint, unrighteous to righteous, tainted to pure.[2]

If we are in Christ, we have been made new and will forever be exploring our newness.

The question we must ask ourselves then, is not whether we have a new nature.

That is not up for debate. Scripture is quite clear on that point.

The question is; are we acting in line with our new God-given nature?

Our new nature affects every part of us, including our minds. If we have renewed minds, then our new minds need to think differently; there must be fresh thought-patterns and mindsets for the renewed mind!

Paul speaks of this in his first letter to the Corinthians:

> *When I was a child, I spoke like a child, I thought like a child, I reasoned like a child. When I became a man, I gave up childish ways.*
> 1 CORINTHIANS 13.11ESV

---

1. *John 3.1-21.*

2. *Ephesians 2* is a good scripture to look at to see how our nature is changed by God's grace.

This chapter is about how we can allow our new, God-given natures affect and shape our minds.

Living Into The Change

Moses experienced a kind of 'second birth' in *Genesis 2.1-10,* similar to the re-birth someone undergoes when they put their faith in Jesus.

He became a 'new person' so to speak.

He was found as a baby by a member of the royal household and adopted into a new family, which just so happened to be that of the King of Egypt, Pharaoh.[3]

Moses was brought up within Pharaoh's household as a prince, raised by Pharaoh's daughter. Even though he was a Hebrew slave by birth, he became Egyptian royalty through adoption.

In order for Moses to fully live into his new life, his new nature, he had to accept that he was now royalty.

Moses' default perceptions of himself, his mindset, needed to change, something he didn't always manage to do.

When Moses murdered an Egyptian slave driver, it is interesting that he did so with an acute awareness of his 'old self'. He was thinking as a Hebrew, who had no authority other than brute force.

But Moses was no longer a Hebrew slave, he was Egyptian royalty.

Perhaps Moses could have used his royal identity to stop the injustice unfolding before him with a single command?

---

3. This part of Moses' story is in *Exodus 2.*

Would the slave drivers have listened to Moses had he ordered them to stop beating the slave using of the authority he had as a member of Pharaoh's household?

But Moses didn't interact with the slave drivers from his position of royalty, and he didn't use his authority to stop the abuse before him.

He used violence instead.

Moses was always designed to lead the Hebrews out of slavery, and it was therefore right for him not to forsake his people in favour of living in Pharaoh's household.[4]

However, God had placed Moses within Pharaoh's household for a reason, and that reason was not murder.

God placed Moses within the Egyptian royal family to be an advocate for His people, eventually leading them out of slavery.

Naturally, God redeemed the situation in *Exodus* and still used Moses to fulfil His plans for His people.

But could it be possible that Moses had the chance to realise God's plan for the Hebrews in another way, acting from his place of royalty, as an honoured son of Pharaoh's daughter?

Staying True To The New You

God always acts perfectly in line with His character.

He is love, and therefore He does loving things.

He is holy, and so all He does is holy.

---

4. *Hebrews 11.24-27.*

He never compromises Himself, and so all He does perfectly reflects who He is.

Part of the joy of following Jesus is that His Spirit's presence within us makes it possible for us to act faithfully to our new nature, just as God acts faithfully to His!

We get to agree with the Spirit working within us, helping us to act in line with the redeemed people that we are.

When we make a mistake or a poor decision, the problem doesn't lie in the fact that we are sinners, because, if we are in Christ Jesus, we are no longer sinners, we are saints.[5]

The issue is why we acted in a way that wasn't true to our new nature.

Everyday we are faced with this same choice in countless guises: whether we live out of the new nature that God has given us, or not.

These choices can be testing because it does not always *feel* like our nature has changed. But, regardless of how we feel about ourselves, or about those around us, the truth is the truth.[6]

It is important to say again here that our new natures in Christ are not static, but are continually unfolding. We have been made new, and are continually being made new.

The same is true for our minds; they have been renewed and yet are continually undergoing renewal:

---

[5]. As I have said before, and will continue to say in this chapter, being a saint does not automatically eliminate the possibility of us making decisions outside of dependence on Jesus.

[6]. *2 Corinthians 5:17*.

> *Do not be conformed to this world, [fashioned after and adapted to its external, superficial customs], but be transformed by the [entire] renewing of your mind [by its new ideals and its new attitude], so that you may prove [for yourselves] what is the good and acceptable and perfect will of God, even the thing which is good and acceptable and perfect [in His sight for you].*
> ROMANS 12.2 AMP

In the book of *Romans*, Paul urges the Christians in Rome to alter the way they think so that it lines up with their new nature.

When Paul encourages his readers to *"be transformed by the renewing of your mind"*, isn't it interesting that He doesn't tell them to *"transform yourself by renewing your mind"*?

In this process of thinking differently, we must remember that God is the source, the maintainer, and the reason for our new nature.

He changed us, and continues to transform us, so that we can be a part of Him, and partner with Him.

If we think we can renew our minds by ourselves, outside of dependence on Him, we are sorely mistaken.

The renewal of our minds does not happen through a human, logical process. It happens through the Spirit's leading.

God is asking you, the you that is only you because of His presence within you, to consider yourself differently and to think differently.

In the next chapter, *Humble Pie*, I will talk more about accepting God's words for us individually, and why it's important to do so; but in this chapter I want to look at what our redeemed, default thought patterns can be, thanks to our new God-given natures.

With our redeemed minds, what are the new thought baselines from which we can live?

What are the beliefs that we can fall back on to help us understand the situations we face?

With our new natures, what Godly conclusions can we now assume?

A Jumpy Mind

The phrase, *"Why did you jump to that conclusion?"*, is commonly used when we feel someone has leapt to an assumption we do not understand.

And just as our minds jump to conclusions in day-to-day life, so the same happens in our walk with Jesus.

Have you considered what your spiritual default ways of thinking are?

And have you considered what default conclusions your mind could now jump to in light of the victory of Jesus Christ?

Through the process of renewal that Paul talks about in *Romans 12*, it is possible for our minds to adopt new default ways of thinking.

For me, the first step in allowing the Spirit to transform my mind, was to leave a fear of making mistakes behind.

I imagine that if you are a bomb disposal expert, you must overcome the fear that the bomb you are working on may detonate in your hands, in order to stand any chance of disarming it.[7]

It is similar for us with our mistakes, or 'sin'. We can be so fearful

---

[7]. By *"overcome the fear"*, I do not mean that the fear disappears, rather that a choice is made to confront something immensely scary in spite of the fear that it brings up.

that our brokenness will explode and ruin us, that we bury it as deep as possible, before we've actually allowed Jesus to minister to us and heal us.

We do not need to be fearful of something that Jesus has paid for.

We get to break free from sin, not hide from it.

In the moments when we do something silly, or find ourselves considering something we don't think we ought to be, we need not run in fear. Instead, we can turn to the Spirit, full of confidence that He is able to explain why we did what we did, and in His ability to transform us.

Instructed by the Holy Spirit, we can see where our minds need to be transformed by Him, and how that would affect our thoughts, actions and behaviour.

We can work with the Holy Spirit to disarm our bad habits and thought patterns.

The Holy Spirit allows certain broken parts of us to rise to the surface, not to shame us, but so that He can explain to us why they are there and begin to heal them.

Jesus' Spirit doesn't *cause* anything un-whole in us, but He wants to make every part of us whole, and so, in His wisdom and perfect timing, He draws different things to the surface at different times.

Through leaving a fear of making mistakes behind us, we open ourselves up for the Spirit to renew us, enabling us to act in accordance with our new natures, and think in line with our redeemed minds.

My Defaults

In the second half of this chapter I would like to give two examples of default ways of thinking that the Holy Spirit is teaching me to adopt and practice in my life.

Over time, God has shown me some new defaults that allow me to stay true to my new nature in any given situation, no matter what happens.

I believe there are many different and unique defaults that God wants to teach us.

We don't all have to call them 'defaults', that is just what I do. Our new, God-given nature is meant to be natural, and so, as we live into our new nature, we will find that our new default ways of thinking become ingrained within us and form our new norm.

As with everything in this book, you are being invited by Jesus to form a completely unique you-and-Him relationship; a relationship that no two people can form other than you being fully you, with God who is always true to Himself.

May these examples from my own life be catalysts used by the Spirit that lead you to thinking in line with the Spirit-filled you.

International Glory

Ben and I were player-managers of A.F.C Bournemouth.

We'd gone through a successful season and gained promotion to the Championship. The night was young, just around 2AM, but alas, we both had work in the morning.

After we'd switched the games console off and watched our dream world of international acclaim slowly float away with the fading power light, we said our goodbyes and Ben trotted down the hill to his house, and I headed to bed.

I climbed between the sheets and closed my eyes, hoping for dreams of FA cup success.

But what I got instead was a torrent of panic.

My mind was suddenly flooded with thoughts such as, *"I've wasted my time by playing this computer game,"* and, *"There is so much more I should be doing with my life instead of gaming."*

So they went on.

I could have thought that this torrent of mental activity was the Holy Spirit trying to tell me that I had been disobedient in playing computer games with Ben. However, would you believe it—and I solemnly promise that this is true—I had received a prophetic word that, for a time, it was good for us to play this particular game together.

In this moment, lying in bed with a flood of accusatory thoughts going through my head, I was reminded about one of the 'defaults' God had taught me.

There Is Never A Need To Panic

As I mentioned earlier in this chapter, we need not bury things that trouble us.

In order for the Holy Spirit to teach us about ourselves, we have to allow Him to put different aspects of us, and our behaviour, into our sightline to study.

In other words, the Holy Spirit uses case studies to explain our hearts to us.

An example of this in my own life was when I went through a six month period where it seemed like most of the things I was doing were going very badly. My faith was struggling, friendships shaky, leadership worrying, and I kept crying.

I just made a string of bad decisions.

At the start of this time, whenever I made a bad decision, I would immediately enter into a cycle of guilt and self-loathing. I got angry with myself, at the part of me that made that decision and I resolutely made plans to avoid making the same mistakes again.

But if I did make the same mistake again, it would all be worse.

Quite early on in this period of time I felt God say to me, *"Don't panic."*

Don't panic?!

I was making decisions I didn't want to make, the people I was leading may have been suffering for it, I'd hurt friends and I'd not been living up to the man I wanted to be.

Gently though, so very gently, the Holy Spirit began to show me why I never need to panic.

You see, God isn't going to throw me overboard if I make a mistake.

There is absolutely nothing I can do that would lead Him to forsake me.[8]

There may be things I do that lead me to forsake Him thinking He has forsaken me, but He will not forsake me.

The Holy Spirit began to show me that He could actually teach me out of making mistakes.

---

8. *Romans 8.38-39.*

Through explaining the reasons behind certain thoughts and actions, God could uncover the incorrect beliefs I had, and correct them. Every mistake I made, the Holy Spirit took as an opportunity for positive change.

The Holy Spirit is astonishingly positive.

He sees every mistake we make as a chance for change, a chance for increased freedom and wholeness.

My tendency to panic had always resulted in me trying to get the ugly parts of myself out of my sight, but the Holy Spirit was bringing them unavoidably *into* my sight.

Once He had taught me not to panic at my mistakes and insecurities, He began freeing me of them. Through allowing the Spirit to delve into my ugliness, He could unknot unhealthy perceptions I had within me.

Because of this new 'default', my post computer game fears became an opportunity to understand myself.

Lying in bed, with the wild thoughts whizzing through my mind, I began to probe for the Holy Spirit.

Sure enough, He was there, wanting to explain what was going on.

You see, that night God changed His blessing on me and Ben playing the computer game. Our time gaming was up and He wanted us to spend our time together in more talkative ways.

I hadn't been disobedient in gaming that night, which was the accusation in my head; but God used my mind to get my attention about His blessing changing for me and for Ben.[9]

---

9. God did not cause the accusatory thoughts in my mind at the time, but He did use them to help me understand that His blessing had changed for me.

If I had listened to the panic in that moment, I would have walked away with the belief that I had been living in disobedience to God for weeks.

Knowing that I never need to panic means that even in times when I don't understand what is going on, or why I'm thinking what I'm thinking, I can peacefully enquire of the Holy Spirit to explain myself to me.

Through not panicking we give ourselves the chance to hear what the Spirit is saying to us in the midst of turmoil, allowing Him to lead us into deeper freedom and fuller life.

There is never a need for panic.

Not a single one.

An Important Note

In the sections above, when I talk about the Holy Spirit bringing things before our eyes to explain them to us, please note that it is vital that we learn to recognise when the Holy Spirit is bringing things before us and when it is just our own accusing mind—or even the Enemy himself.

It is all too easy for us to bring to mind every single mistake, worrying thought and insecurity, and try to solve them all at once ourselves.

In my experience, the Holy Spirit doesn't do things 'all at once' very often.

Sometimes He does, and that is of course to be celebrated with all we've got within us.

But I have more commonly seen God work within His people over time, correcting and healing them.

If we try to bring up everything we want solving at once, we may well become overwhelmed and feel bad about ourselves.

It's best to allow the Holy Spirit to bring things up in His time, when He knows it is best to deal with them!

I Can Trust Myself

The other example of a default that God has spoken to me about for my life that I would like to talk through is, 'I can trust myself'.

It's my absolute favourite.

Before I start though, because this one is perhaps the easiest to misunderstand, please can we remind ourselves of one thing?

When I am talking of 'myself', I am referring to the new me, the redeemed me with the credited righteousness of Jesus. The me that is only me because I am in partnership with the Holy Spirit who resides within me, thanks to the blood of Christ.

I'm talking about me with, not without, God.

That's important to understand.

As people filled with God's Holy Spirit, with hearts God has made soft again[10], and whose minds have been transformed into the mind of Christ[11], we can trust the new us.

Those who have been born again are holy, pure and righteous.

That means we can be trustworthy people, with trustworthy hearts and trustworthy minds.

---

10. *Ezekiel 11.19 & 36.26.*
11. *1 Corinthians 2.16.*

If we do not truly believe the work of Christ in our lives, we will always be battling against our new hearts and minds, thinking them sinful and dark parts of us.

They used to be, but they aren't any more.

This does not mean that our minds and hearts aren't capable of feeling and thinking bad things.

As I've said previously, we all have daily choices whether we act in accordance with our new God-given natures, or not.

We are still able to act and think as if we haven't been given a new heart and mind, but we have the choice to learn how to live faithfully to our God-given hearts of flesh and minds of Christ.

As long as we're not doing something in spite of the Spirit's conviction, a conviction that can be clearly seen in Scripture, as well as in impressions and feelings, I believe we can act in good faith that God is for what we are doing.

This is because as we grow closer and closer to Jesus, He changes our hearts so that they start reflecting parts of His.

We begin wanting what He wants.

Being able to identify and trust what God has placed in our hearts is crucial!

> *I will bless the Lord, who has given me counsel: yes, my heart instructs me in the night seasons.*
> PSALM 16.7 AMP

In this *Psalm*, David is celebrating the fact that God guides him through his heart.[12]

---

12. Biblically *"the heart"* does not just refer to our feelings. *"The heart" (cont. on next page)*

If we don't trust our hearts, we may well be missing guid. from God!

For me, it came as quite a revelation that what I felt and thought may not always be bad.

That I could actually trust myself.

Again, I'm not condoning us justifying any wanton desires and feelings; we need to have real integrity in this. I am talking about the desires that are pleasing to God, and could well be from God.

When we cannot hear God externally, instead of feeling like God has abandoned us, we may need to look at His voice set inside of us, just as David did in *Psalm 16*.

I know that our hearts can throw a real cocktail of emotions and feelings at us, but we have the Spirit within us to help us discern what is good, and what is bad.

And just as our redeemed hearts can be trusted, so can our renewed minds!

Romans 12.2 tells us that through our minds being renewed, we can find out what is pleasing to God.

We can find truth in our thoughts.

Within our minds and hearts, God has hidden guidance from Him, for us and for others.

---

has a far stronger meaning than that—it is an inner voice communicating to us, similar to our conscience.

Thanks To God

you?

think your new defaults are, thanks to the work of Christ in your life.

They will be specific to you, things that you find life-giving and releasing.

Perhaps it is that you have the authority of heaven, or that you can always approach God in anything, in the midst of any situation?

Maybe a new default for you is that you never need to react from a place of fear, or that God is for you?

We are able to have our default settings reset by the Spirit because Jesus has made us new.

And a new mind will think new thoughts.

If we don't move with our newness, we will disregard good things that God has planted within us.

If we panic at the first sign of brokenness within us, then we will not allow the Spirit to explain what is happening to us, or let Him help us become increasingly free and healthy people.

Always remember that God is the best leader in what He has to teach you. We may see good ideas in those around us, but unless God is breathing on them for our ears, they aren't always worth hearing.

You have the chance for new defaults, starting points, baselines or whatever else you may call them.

Will you journey with the Holy Spirit to find out what they are, helping yourself to live according to your new God-given nature?

8.
HUMBLE PIE

You sit here
(whether you like it or not.)

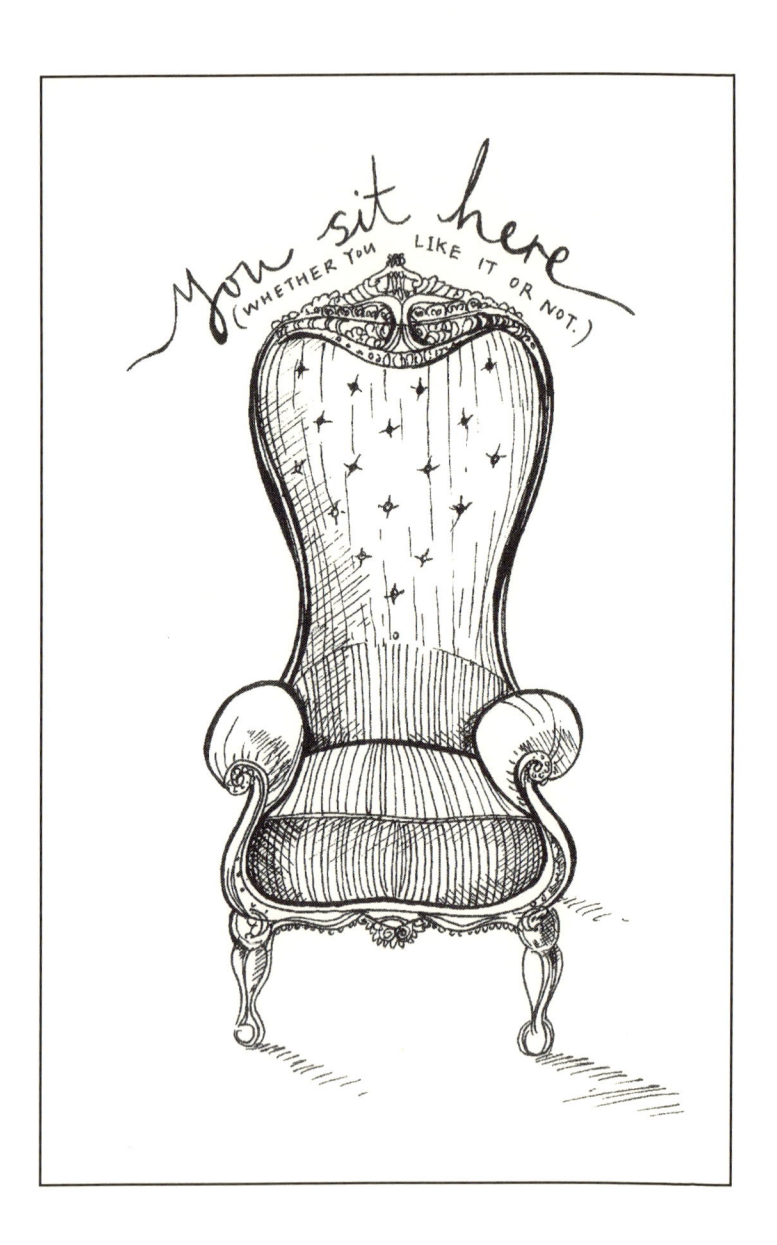

Humility As A Response

Humility is a key part of the Christian life, and is a character trait that Scripture encourages every believer to pursue.

Because humility is such an important subject, it is important that we understand what true, godly humility is, to make sure that we are each pursuing the humility that Jesus modelled.

The first thing to note about godly humility is that it is linked to a specific environment:

> *Clothe yourselves, all of you, with humility toward one another, for 'God opposes the proud but gives grace to the humble.'*
>
> *Humble yourselves, therefore, under the mighty hand of God so that at the proper time he may exalt you.*
> 1 PETER 5.5B-6 ESV
>
> *Humble yourselves before the Lord, and he will exalt you.*
> JAMES 4.10 ESV

When Peter tells his readers to *"humble themselves"*, there is a context within which the humbling occurs: *"under the mighty hand of God"*.

Peter doesn't just tell his readers to humble themselves and leave them to it, because it is an impossible task to achieve unless it is done within a specific setting.

The only place that godly humility can be nurtured and grown is in God's presence.

Imagine that someone gave you a bag of garden peas and asked you to freeze them without using a freezer or ice. It would be hard to do.

This is because peas freeze as a natural reaction to the environment created in a freezer.

What happens to a pea when it is in a freezer?

It becomes a frozen pea.

What happens to a soft-hearted person when they're in God's presence?

They grow in humility.[1]

Humility cannot grow within us unless we put ourselves in front of God, because godly humility only grows as a response to Him.

If we think that humility is merely having the ability to laugh at ourselves, or to acknowledge that we aren't terribly good at some things, or even that we make poor choices sometimes, we are sorely mistaken.

That is like trying to freeze peas by just willing them to freeze.

If we pursue that kind of self-invented humility, we may either become proud inside, thinking we are achieving humility, or enter into a cycle of deep self-loathing, thinking it necessary in order to obtain humility.

Humility is not the ability to regularly find flaws and imperfections in ourselves.

I've seen people choose to accept insecurities because they think it is their 'thorn in the flesh', there to keep them humble.

---

1. As with most analogies, my frozen pea one does have its floors. A pea cannot choose whether it freezes in a freezer, whereas you and I can choose to be soft-hearted or hard-hearted towards God, which will affect whether we grow in humility when we're in His presence.

But God does not need us to have insecurities to keep us humble.

He is glorious enough that He Himself is sufficient to create true humility within all people.

As ever, Jesus is our go-to example for the Christian life as it can be lived, and He did not live agreeing and accepting lies about Himself in order to be 'humble'.

Therefore, neither do we.

Getting Ready For The Light

Our bodies do a whole host of things sub-consciously.

Breathing, digesting and sweating are just a few of the marvels that are happening inside of us all the time, without our conscious effort.

Some of the subconscious things we do happen as a reaction to an external stimulant or environment; like the reflex of rapidly pulling a hand back if we were to touch something burning hot, or the dilation and contraction of our pupils depending on the amount of light reaching them.

Imagine having to consciously prepare your pupil when you were about to enter a room brighter, or darker, than the one you were just leaving.

Imagine if you had to get your pupil's dilation exactly right before entering the room in order to be able to see well.

It would be incredibly hard.

You might manage it by chance on the odd occasion, but the rest of the time you'd be a bit off, and unable to see very well. It's a good thing our eyes react naturally to the light around us.

I think that our own attempts at growing in humility are similar to us trying to pre-empt the effect of light on our eyes.

It's unnecessary and can be woefully inaccurate.

I believe that humility begins as a reaction to the presence, and the persons, of God.

Reactions, by their very nature, are natural.

They just happen.

If we don't choose to place ourselves before God and open up to Him with all that is inside of us, we cannot find true humility.

When Peter writes *"humble yourself under the mighty hand of God"*, I believe he is telling his readers to put themselves before God.

To submit themselves to being in God's presence.

Not a grumpy, slouching-into-the-room-putting-myself-before-You, attitude, but an eager, I'm-bringing-everything-I-am-when-I-enter-Your-presence, attitude.

When we put ourselves before God, we see whatever aspect of His character He wants to reveal in that moment.

And whatever aspect of His character He reveals will lead to humility flourishing within us.

How on earth can we second-guess which aspect of God's many-sided wisdom we need to heed in our hearts in any given moment, in order to grow in humility?

Best to leave it to Him.

Humility grows in us as a reaction to witnessing the glory of God.

It's a reaction.

We just need to walk into the light, and it happens.

Only The Half Of It

The word 'humble' is defined in *The Concise Oxford Dictionary* as:

"Having a low estimate of one's importance."[2]

The issue I have with this definition of humility is that it places your opinion of yourself as the most important one.

It encourages you to form a low or modest opinion of yourself.

But your voice isn't the most important voice.

Surely Godly humility is about believing what God says about you no matter what?

To lay aside your self-perceptions so that God can fill you with His perception of the redeemed you?

And what you and I will find when we do this, is that God actually thinks very highly of us.

He gave His son to die for us.

To hold onto a low self-perception in light of how highly God values each of us begins to look insulting.

God didn't choose us because of our effort to look good, or because of our ability to be modest.

---

2. 'Humble' Def.1a. *The Concise Oxford Dictionary*. 8th ed. 1991. Print.

God chose us because He wanted to.[3]

Do you see?

He chose you and paid the highest price for you because He values you so highly.

To keep on living in a self-condemning mindset throws God's valuation of you right back in His face.

I don't think we should re-examine humility because *we're* amazing but because *He* is amazing.

In accepting Jesus, His nature has more than just rubbed off on us—it has changed us and now indwells us!

I want to think of myself in no other way than the way He thinks of me, and it just so happens that He thinks of me incredibly highly and fondly.

If our view of ourselves matched God's view of us, then we would live fully content in the fact that we are loved by Him, and we would love the way God has made us.

Not a love of self that is arrogant or self-seeking, but a pure, godly love, rooted in and stemming from God's love for us.

One of the greatest commands Jesus gave was to *"love your neighbour as yourself"*[4], which requires a godly love of self, in order to love those around us.

According to Jesus, the level to which we love ourselves is the level to which we can love our neighbours.

---

3. *John 15.16.*
4. *Mark 12.31.*

If you think lowly of yourself, then you will not be able to truly think highly of others, in a godly way.

You'll become jealous of them, or idolise them.

Jesus Himself was wholly compassionate and loving to the world around Him in a perfectly godly manner, and so holding Him up to His own teaching, He must have loved Himself fully.

Perhaps we could also read *1 Corinthians 13* with a mirror in front of us and see how much we are acting out of love for ourselves?

Even when we get angry or make mistakes.

We must refuse to define ourselves according to our perception of ourselves over God's perception of us.

God will never think of us more or less highly than He does any other person.

So if we give ourselves to seeing ourselves as He sees us, we need not fear that in agreeing with His opinion of us we will become proud.

God, in His grace, mercy, kindness and goodness, has made us powerful, significant co-heirs with Christ.

Who are we to disagree?

What Tears Us Away?

Before moving on to look at some biblical individuals who display true humility, I would like to talk briefly about what can tear us away from being humble.

Pride is the opposite of humility, but it is not always pride that tears us away from humility.

We can also be torn away by disappointment, success or any other of life's events, emotions or trials.

Instead of trying to avoid any emotion that could draw us away from humility, why don't we just stay close to the Father in the knowledge that His presence will grow and form humility within us?

When we wander away from the Father it is not always rebuke that brings us near again.

Sometimes what we need to be brought back to true humility is a revelation of God's evergreen goodness.

Sometimes we need a reality check.

For too long some have reduced God's path to humility as one of rebuke, embarrassment or discipline.

I've no doubt that sometimes we may need a rebuke and discipline from God in order to grow in humility. However, I also have no doubt that a sudden, overwhelming, emotional encounter with the kindness and loving nature of Jesus will also lead us to humility.

Let God choose the best path to lead each of us back to Him and further into humility.

Let us not take it upon ourselves to second guess how the Father intends to grow humility in us.

I assure you that our methods to nurture humility within ourselves will not compare to the perfect ways of the Father.

Gideon

I'd like us to look at three characters from the Bible I believe displayed true, godly humility.

Gideon, Mary the mother of Jesus and King David.

Firstly, Gideon.

Gideon meets the Angel of the Lord under an oak tree whilst he is threshing wheat in a wine press to hide it from some invaders.[5]

The Angel says that God calls Gideon *"courageous"*.

But Gideon is hiding his food in a wine press because he is fearful of Israel's enemy...?

God goes on to ask Gideon to go out and conquer that enemy.

Gideon replies that he is from the least of all the houses in the area, and, on top of that, he is the least in his family.

God calls Gideon mighty and Gideon tries to tell God that he is the weakest of the weak.

According to the *The Concise Oxford Dictionary's* definition of humility, Gideon should receive a rapturous round of applause for his humble, low view of himself.

But God's response to Gideon's low estimate of his importance is not to congratulate Gideon on his 'humility'.

Gideon cannot be displaying true humility, because what Gideon is displaying is getting in the way of God's will for him.

Yes, Gideon's fear and low opinion of himself presented God with an opportunity to demonstrate His glory, which He duly did, but the fact that God used Gideon to demonstrate His glory does not mean that Gideon's fear and low self-worth were godly.

---

5. You can find this in *Judges 6.11-16*.

Think of the story of Joseph when, many years after his brothers had attempted to murder him, he says to them:

> *As for you, you meant evil against me, but God meant it for good, to bring it about that many people should be kept alive, as they are today.*
> GENESIS 50.20 ESV

Despite people agreeing with, or doing something that is not of God, God can still transform that ungodly thing into something glorious.

It doesn't make the initial ungodly motive godly though.

It just demonstrates God's redemptive power.

So it was with Gideon.

God was not stopped by Gideon's insecurities, but that doesn't mean that Gideon's insecurities were good!

God uses broken people all the time, and He is superb at doing so; however, let us remind ourselves that the most fruitful life ever lived was that of Jesus Christ and He had no insecurities and committed no sin.

Brokenness does not stop God from using us, but God does not need us to be broken *in order* to use us—He just needs us to be obedient in following Him.

After God has told Gideon to, *"Go in this might of yours and save Israel from the hand of Midian,"*[6] Gideon has an important choice to make.

God has declared who He sees Gideon to be, and Gideon has to choose whether to believe God's word about him, or not.

---

6. *Judges 6.14b.*

He's humbled through his conversation with the Lord's Angel enough to realise that if God believes he is a mighty and courageous man, then that must be true, even though he doesn't feel it.

And so he walks out with God to conquer the enemy.[7]

Mary

Mary, the mother of Jesus, is one of my wife's favourite Bible characters.

As a very young, engaged woman, Mary meets an angel who tells her that she will become pregnant with God's own Son.[8]

Mary asks a logistical question, which leads to the angel telling her that she will be made pregnant by the Holy Spirit.

Right.

Mary's response?

"I'm really sorry to let you down, but I'm not worthy to parent the only child God is to ever have, and so I don't believe you and won't be arrogant enough to presume that you were being serious."

Obviously not her response.

What she does say is:

> 'Behold, I am the servant of the Lord; let it be to me according to your word.' And the angel departed from her.
> LUKE 1.38 ESV

---

7. For the full story read *Judges 6.11-7.25*.
8. *Luke 1.26-38*.

Humble Pie

Of course Mary wasn't worthy to carry Jesus. No one would have been.

But that wasn't the point.

The point was that God deemed her worthy.

He chose her because that is what He chose to do.

She decided to listen to God's voice over her own.

She was a truly humble person.

Believing that God has called us to do something great does not automatically mean that we have stopped being humble!

Mary played a crucial role in the greatest event ever recorded in history because she chose to believe that what God said He intended to do through her, was possible.

Her choice to believe that she could be part of something truly great speaks of her humility.

Mary didn't go and rub it in everyone's faces that she had been chosen, or that she was special.

She knew that it was God's choice to use her, not a result of her own effort, and so she set about living into the word of God for her life, quietly and faithfully.

She pondered it in her heart.[9]

---

9. *Luke 2.19.*

King David

Like Gideon, David was the least in his family, as he was the youngest child, yet God asked Samuel the prophet to anoint this young shepherd boy as the future King of Israel.[10]

David then had to live believing this word over him for many years before it actually came to pass. He didn't become a self-obsessed fool, proclaiming that he was to be king; he just continually gave himself into God's hands, trusting and believing God's word for him until it happened.

When he did at last become king, David wrote the following psalm:

> *The King [David] shall enjoy in Your strength, O Lord; and in Your salvation how greatly shall he rejoice!*
>
> *You have given him his hearts desire and have not withheld the request of his lips. Selah [Pause, and think of that]!*
>
> *For You send blessings of good things to meet him; You set a crown of pure gold on his head.*
>
> *He asked life of You, and You gave it to him – long life for ever and evermore.*
>
> *His glory is great because of Your aid; splendour and majesty You bestow upon him.*
>
> *For You make him to be blessed and a blessing for ever; You make him exceedingly glad with the joy of Your presence.*
>
> *For the King trusts, relies on, and is confident in the Lord, and through the mercy and steadfast love of the Most High he will*

---

10. *1 Samuel 16.1-13.*

Humble Pie

himself to believing God's word about him, that things about himself such as, *"You make him to ...ssed and a blessing forever,"* and, *"His glory is great because of Your aid."*

Can you imagine someone singing next to you in church about how God has, *"Made their glory great,"* and how they've been, *"Made to be blessed and a blessing for ever?"*

I think perhaps most of us would be offended if we heard someone speaking of themselves like that. But you see, it was actually wholly right for King David to be saying those things.

King David understood that if God had decided to make him king of a nation, and to give him riches and power, David was to agree with God's word.

To try and continually deny his significance or glory as king would have been irresponsible, and the opposite of humility!

What we see in Gideon, Mary and David are the two characteristics of true humility.

Firstly, it is believing what God says about you *in spite* of what you may believe about yourself.

It's not ignoring what you believe about yourself—you must work through insecurities and fears you have with God so that He can change your self-perception to match His perception of you.

It is believing that what God says about you is the truth, no matter whether big or small, simple or earth-shatteringly-complex. You need to let His word about you replace your opinion about yourself.

His word over you can become your word over you.

His perception of you can be your perception of you.

Secondly, it is not letting the word God has given to you lead you out of communion with Him.

As I've already said, humility is a response to God and we meet with God by being in His presence. If we allow God's word about us to draw us away from Him, either through believing that we can fulfil His word without Him, or through believing that we can't possibly achieve His word even with Him, then we have distanced ourselves from the source of true humility.

Privilege And Purpose

The two characteristics I mentioned at the end of the last section, about believing in God's word, and remaining in communion with Him, can be summarised by the words 'privilege' and 'purpose'.

A person with true humility carries a continual sense of privilege at being loved, transformed and used by God.

What we see in Gideon, Mary and King David is that they didn't take God's word for them as a right. They remained amazed and ever thankful that God had chosen them.

King David did step outside of this sense of privilege at times and he made some poor decisions. When he slept with Bathsheba[11], or took a census of Israel[12], he allowed himself to act outside of communion with God.

---

11. *2 Samuel 11.*

12. *2 Samuel 24.*

He began to claim rights that were outside of God's desire for him.

He became proud.

Humility starts with that sense of, 'Who, me?' as God calls us, firstly to know Him, and secondly into whatever works He wants to do with us. That sense of gratitude at being chosen need never leave our hearts.

Holding onto that sense of privilege is essential to being a person of humility.

However, Gideon, Mary and King David also all had a great sense of purpose.

They decided to believe that God could truly use them and they took God's word seriously. They set aside their disbelief at being chosen, and lived into God's purposes for them.

Having a sense of privilege and a strong sense of purpose are two sides of humility.

It's easy to believe that humility is just acknowledging that we don't deserve relationship with God because of our sin.

That used to be true, but for those who are in Christ, God has moved us beyond our sin.

He might use that sudden realisation of our neediness to bring us to Him, but He then always calls us higher and to greater things.

Not to make us proud or arrogant, but because He is on a mission and He has decided to work with you and me!

We need to ask whether we are willing to truly believe whatever God is saying to us and about us, above what we believe about ourselves.

Are we willing to become truly humble?

The Ever-Present Words Of God

So far I have focused mainly on humility being about believing the specific words God has given to us for our individual lives; where He says He intends to do things with us beyond our wildest dreams, and declares who He sees us to be.

However, God also presents us with a list of incredible truths in Scripture.

In Scripture, God says that we are His righteousness.[13]

Saints, not sinners.[14]

Holy.[15]

Blameless.[16]

Pure.[17]

Sanctified.[18]

Co-heirs with Christ.[19]

Full of God Himself.[20]

The list goes on.

---

13. *2 Corinthians 5.21.*
14. *1 Corinthians 1.2.*
15. *Colossians 1.22.*
16. *Jude 1.24 & Revelation 14.5.*
17. *Isaiah 1.18.*
18. *1 Corinthians 6.11 & Hebrews 10.10.*
19. *Romans 8.17.*
20. *1 Corinthians 3.16 & 2 Timothy 1.14.*

I encourage you to read through the New Testament and to take heed of every single one of the declarations made about our new nature as Christians.

Make a note of them.

It takes incredible humility to wholeheartedly believe that these things about us are true when we are all too aware of our short-comings, mistakes and errors.

For some reason we've decided that calling ourselves 'sinners' is the path to having a 'godly', low self-worth.

If God hadn't given us the Scriptures, we would have little choice but to keep thinking of ourselves as lowly sinners.

But God has spoken.

He says that we're not sinners any more.

I know that we don't feel like saints all of the time. In fact, perhaps we don't feel like a saint much of the time. But the reality is, that in spite of what we feel and do, the truth is the truth.

Will we humble ourselves to believe it?

Believe it to such an extent that we actually see ourselves as saints?

Holy and blameless?

Not to claim any credit for ourselves, but rather to give all credit to Jesus.

Humility From A Place Of Power

In this chapter I have explained how godly humility grows within us as a natural reaction to meeting God.

As we walk out our lives with Him, He imparts His opinion of us onto us, so that it gradually becomes our opinion of ourselves.

So that we see ourselves as God sees us.

God sees us as powerful people. We are in-dwelt by God's Spirit and given all authority.

We could be no more powerful.

This reality can make us feel uncomfortable.

I think that one of the reasons we have been hesitant to see ourselves as the powerful saints God has redeemed us to be, is because we don't want to lose our conscious need for God.

Perhaps we think that if we get too powerful we will walk away from God, thinking we do not need Him, or that we will be less in awe of His goodness and grace.

The perfect model of humility is, of course, Jesus, and Paul wonderfully explains how Jesus went about being humble in *Philippians 2*:

> *Who, though He was in the form of God, did not count equality with God a thing to be grasped,*
>
> *but emptied Himself, by taking the form of a servant, being born in the likeness of men.*
>
> *And being found in human form, He humbled Himself by becoming obedient to the point of death, even death on a cross.*

> *Therefore God has highly exalted Him and bestowed on Him the name that is above every name,*
>
> *so that at the name of Jesus every knee should bow, in heaven and on earth and under the earth,*
>
> *and every tongue confess that Jesus Christ is Lord, to the glory of God the Father.*
> PHILIPPIANS 2.6-11 ESV

One of the incredible things about Jesus was that His all-powerful nature did not result in Him becoming proud.

Quite the reverse—it led Him to choose humility.

Jesus chose to let God's words and plans for Him define what He did, even though He was all-powerful.

It cannot be true therefore, that we need to shun the idea of being powerful and continually remind ourselves of our 'sinfulness' in order to be humble.

That would have been impossible for Jesus to live out, because He never sinned.

Humility is its most true when it is chosen from a place of power, not a place of weakness.

Humility is about us believing God, but also it's about choosing to submit ourselves completely to Him.

Believing that He has made us powerful saints, but choosing to submit this powerful new nature to His purposes and plans.

It is really just imitating Christ.

We need to surrender our ways of trying to keep ourselves humble and give ourselves to God's way of keeping us humble.

We can lower our self-opinion to try to remain humble, but Scripture tell us that God has exalted us to sit with Him in the heavenly realm and invites us to submit our grace-given authority to serve Him.[21]

I believe that Jesus chose to submit His life to God because He knew, by experience, how good, wonderful, lovely, amazing and glorious God is.

I believe it is possible for us to so love God that we will always want to choose to submit our new God-given nature to His purposes.

Humbling ourselves under His mighty hand.

---

21. *Ephesians 2.6.*

9.
IT'S ALWAYS TIME FOR YOUR DANCING SHOES

the ever-present reason to dance

The Dross Of Karaoke

I wanted to get to know Tom a little better and so we went to a café one afternoon to chat and spend time together.

One of the things I was immediately drawn to in Tom, was his refreshing freedom to articulate thoughts and feelings that some Christians might avoid for fear of being heard to be saying the 'wrong thing'.

Quite quickly we got onto the topic of sung worship, as it happened to be something that Tom was quite frustrated with at the time.

During the conversation he said to me, *"It feels as if we are just doing karaoke in church."*

He went on to explain that he felt this because during times of sung worship, lyrics appear on the screen and we sing along because it's the 'right thing to do'.

And when a favourite song is played we sing all the louder, and perhaps throw an arm in the air as a mark of our enthusiasm.

Tom was dissatisfied with sung worship being like this.

It didn't appeal to him in the slightest and there was something within him telling him that this surely wasn't what worship was meant to be about.

Of course, Tom knew that people do truly worship through singing songs with words on a screen. His issue wasn't anything to do with the practice of sung worship; it was the underlying attitudes and beliefs that can be present within sung worship.

He wasn't articulating a general doubt or cynicism at the place of worship in the church, he was just not satisfied with what worship can sometimes become.

His words stuck with me;

"It feels as if we are doing karaoke in church."

Mere karaoke.

The Age-Old Issue

My chat with Tom left me pondering a question: why do we engage in sung worship as we do?

Like Tom, I do not want to question the tradition of sung worship in the church, but I do want to encourage each of us to look at our own approaches, beliefs and attitudes towards sung worship.

I also want to make it clear from the start that worship is a whole-life attitude and practice. We worship God first and foremost with our lives, as well as expressing worship in song and through music.

However, I want to focus on sung worship because of its central role in our churches. Whether we like it or not, sung worship plays a pivotal part within many churches and has the ability to inspire, or to put off, members of the church.

What Tom was getting at, and what stuck with me, was how easy it is for us to just sing along during times of sung worship because it seems like the right thing to do. We put songs into a church service plan because it's become our routine; it's what we've always done.

Underneath it all, we know that sung worship is about coming before God and praising Him, giving our all to Him and acknowledging who He is.

We know He deserves it, that Scripture encourages it, and we know that sometimes He is gracious enough to make His presence among us tangible, which really blows us away.

But all too often we keep this knowledge in our heads as we come to sung worship.

We know that praising God is the correct thing to do, and so we do it, regardless of how we're feeling, or whether it feels like truth to us in that moment.

In fact, when our hearts don't *feel* like worshipping, we can, and I believe we have sometimes been encouraged to, actively shut them down, so that we can 'choose to worship' in spite of them, without seeking to understand *why* our hearts don't feel excited at the prospect of worshipping Jesus.

I'm not suggesting that we should wait for our hearts to be feeling perfectly positive before we worship; God is always worthy to be praised in spite of every imaginable trying circumstance or painful situation.

Yet the truth that He is worthy of praise no matter what we are feeling, does not necessarily mean that what we are feeling is unimportant, insignificant or not an essential part of a healthy life of worship.

I imagine that most of us *know* that God delights in true worship— worship offered from the heart, over religious acts of worship— offering God something from a place of duty; but do we actually know how to worship God from our hearts when they aren't feeling inspired and moved by God?

Fortunately, this is not a new issue.

Throughout Scripture we see God's people doing and saying the 'right things' before Him. But God's response to these offerings is to ask for the hearts of His people.

He doesn't want His people just to say and do the 'right things'.

Isaiah 29 is a great example of this:

> *And the Lord said:*
> *'Because this people draw near with their mouth*
> *and honour me with their lips,*
> *while their hearts are far from me,*
> *and their fear of me is a commandment taught by men,*
>
> *therefore, behold, I will again*
> *do wonderful things with this people,*
> *with wonder upon wonder;*
> *and the wisdom of their wise men shall perish,*
> *and the discernment of their discerning men shall be hidden.'*
> ISAIAH 29.13-14 ESV

God is telling His people that He sees them 'worshipping' Him outwardly, but that He can also see that their hearts are not involved in the worship. They are doing what they know to be 'right', praising God with their lips, without bringing all of themselves to the worship.

The line that really sticks out to me is; *"And their fear of me is a commandment taught by men."*

The Israelites' fear of God wasn't in response to a personal knowledge of Him, their fear was a commandment, a rule, that they had been told to obey by others.

How easy is it to sing praises to God purely because we have been told to, because we have been taught that He deserves it?

The people of God had been told to fear God because it is a right and appropriate response to who He is. But without that reaction to Him coming from their hearts, it was just an empty practice!

So what was God's response to people worshipping Him solely because it is what they had been taught to do, without their hearts being involved?

*therefore, behold, I will again
do wonderful things with this people,
with wonder upon wonder;
and the wisdom of their wise men shall perish,
and the discernment of their discerning men shall be hidden.*
ISAIAH 29.14 ESV

He decided to demonstrate His wonders to them.

Why?

So that the lessons people had been taught by human teachers could be relearnt as a heartfelt response to God Himself.

It is true that God deserves to be praised. He is always worthy, glorious and gracious.

But instead of telling people what they ought to do and how they should behave towards Him, what would happen if we let God Himself demonstrate to people how wonderful He is and see what their natural response would be?

What if God would rather we didn't tell people what they *should* do, but instead provide an environment where they can meet with Him in such a way that He can reveal what He desires for them Himself?

The Cost

2 Samuel 24 is one of the go-to scriptures for teaching on worship.

King David has just taken a census to see how many people there are in Israel, but this was in disobedience to God's specific word to David. God convicts David and sends a man called Gad to tell him to go and offer a sacrifice on the threshing floor of Araunah the Jebusite.[1]

---

1. Read the full story in *1 Samuel 24*.

Araunah sees King David coming and offers David all he needs for the sacrifice, free of cost.

The land, the wood, the animal, everything:

> *But the King said to Araunah, 'No, but I will buy it from you for a price. I will not offer burnt offerings to the Lord my God that cost me nothing.' So David bought the threshing floor and the oxen for fifty shekels of silver.*
> 2 SAMUEL 24.24 ESV

From this scripture comes the teaching that worship must cost us something; that there needs to be a sacrifice involved in worship.

However, we have to take into account that David actually *wanted* his worship to cost him something.

I don't think he had to consult his mind to work out what the right response in that minute was.

He was offered the means for worship at no cost and his *reaction* was a resounding *"no"*!

He didn't *want* to worship God if it cost him nothing.

It didn't feel right to him.

Now I'm sure some might say that King David may have known in advance that Araunah was likely to offer the land and sacrifice materiel to him for free, so he had time to prepare his response.

But the fact remains that it was David's desire not to give something to God that cost him nothing.

It was his desire that led him to his decision to pay Araunah for the threshing floor, rather than a sense of religious duty or obligation.

Jesus sheds further light on this in *Mark 12.41-44*, when He observes a widow's financial offering in contrast to some rich people's offerings.

The rich people in *Mark 12* were 'giving', and so their worship was undoubtedly 'costing' them something. But their hearts were not truly in their giving. Although their giving *looked* magnificent to those watching, and probably made them feel great in themselves, to God, their giving was empty.

If their hearts had been in their giving, their act of worship, then they would not have seen financial giving as a religious obligation to be practiced; they would have seen it as an opportunity to express the deep love within them for their God.

Jesus did not highlight the widow because she gave a higher proportion of what she had[2], He commented on her because her love for God led her to give, irrespective of the cost.[3]

Physically, the Pharisees gave more money, but they actually gave less of themselves.

The widow gave less money, but in actual fact, her offering was worth more.

The significant difference between the widow and rich people was not what percentage of their finances they gave to God; the difference was how much they loved God and that love was demonstrated in what they gave.

The widow so loved God that she *wanted* to give everything.

Her duty was to give God a portion of what she had, but her passion led her to give *all* she had to God.

---

2. Even though she did give a higher proportion—she gave all she had; 100% of what she owned.

3. *Mark 12.41-44.*

Duty will never lead us to give nearly as much as love does.

The call to grow in worship is not about trying and grow in the amount we give.

The invitation is to grow in our heart-felt love for God, which will lead us to grow in what we give in worship.

All too often we try to force ourselves to worship in spite of our hearts, wanting to imitate King David in choosing to offer God worship that costs us;

Costs us our dignity, our feeling of safety or our comfort.

In moments when we don't really feel like we want to worship, we resolutely ignore the state of our hearts so that we can force ourselves to sing the songs and say the words.

We don't stop and ask the question;

"Why don't I want to worship?"

The cost of worship is not to bury our feelings and fears so we can to choose to articulate praise; it is to bring ourselves wholly before God.

The real cost of worship is to stop hiding from God:

> *But the hour is coming, and is now here, when the true worshipers will worship the Father in spirit and truth, for the Father is seeking such people to worship him.*
> JOHN 4.23 ESV

You see God is seeking true worshippers.

People who worship in a way that is true to themselves, true to how they are and who they are.

People who come with all of themselves, all of the time, willing for God to minister to their hearts no matter what they are feeling.

As they are, in the moment.

I believe that the way we can engage in worship in a true, wholehearted manner, is to bring our hearts before God with all of their feelings and emotions at every given moment.

We do not bring our hearts before God to justify our emotions, but to give Him the permission and the opportunity to change them. We bring our hearts to God because we want them to be so ignited by God, that they explode with praise.

This is why in *Isaiah 29.13-14* God remedies religion with a demonstration of Himself in all of His wonder.

God knows that people will truly and purely worship Him, when they see Him.

God invites us to come before Him free from obligation, unshackled from religious duty, so that we can bring all of ourselves into His presence free from any pressure to act in the 'correct way'. And as we come before Him, He ministers to us in the perfect way, as only He can.

The result?

Love for God blossoms within us like a well watered flower in sunlight.

For love always leads to action.

And so this love for God that grows within us as we encounter Him, bursts out in worship.

Before we know it, the very things we were trying to force ourselves to do in order to act 'appropriately' before God, we find ourselves doing naturally as our heart-felt love for Him bubbles over.

In fact, just like the widow from *Mark 12.41-44*, we will find ourselves naturally going far *beyond* what we had been taught was the suitable response to God.

In order for us to respond to God truly, we must be true to ourselves; true to ourselves in that moment before God, trusting that He will minister to us in such a way that we will be left with an irrepressible desire to praise.

If you come to sung worship and find yourself not wanting to participate, don't just force yourself to dance, or sing as loudly as you can.

Instead, ask God why;

"Why don't I want to worship?"

Bring before God your feelings and your thoughts. Allow Him to direct you and free you into explosive praise.

Give Him the chance to explain you to you, and to slowly undo you, until you find yourself wanting to worship again, and again, and again.

The Worship Cycle

I have said a number of times that worship happens as a response to God. When we see and experience Him in our lives, it inspires us to worship.

Through talking with Him when we aren't feeling excited about worship, instead of just forcing ourselves to worship in spite of how we are, we invite God to minister to us.

His Spirit gently comes and washes over us so that our hurts and frustrations aren't buried, but are resolved. As our hearts are encouraged and helped, we find ourselves inspired to thank God in worship.

Our worship is a response to His activity.

But did we know that our worship also inspires His activity?

In *2 Chronicles 5.13* and *2 Chronicles 7.2-3*, the cloud of God's presence manifests to the people of Israel. In other words, the people of Israel could feel, and in this case see, God's presence around them.

It's interesting to note *when* the cloud comes in each of these scriptures. Not so we can try and trick God into making His presence tangible, but to better understand the cyclical nature of worship.

In *2 Chronicles 5*, the people of Israel are celebrating the construction of the temple, planned by King David, completed by his son, King Solomon. The ark of the covenant is brought into the temple and the people begin to celebrate in song.

They have witnessed God's faithfulness, from the dream of the temple that David had, to its fulfilment under Solomon. They're overwhelmed by God's goodness and sing:

> *He is good, for His mercy and loving-kindness endure forever*
> 2 CHRONICLES 5.13B AMP

Just after they start singing, the cloud of God's presence arrives and they can't sing any more.

You see, when we are whole-heartedly worshipping, true to ourselves and fully before God, we're giving God the invitation to meet with us and to change us.

We encounter the reality of God through true worship.

But then later, Solomon prays a dedication prayer over the finished temple and the cloud comes back. This time it is the cloud that inspires the people into sung worship![4]

---

4. *2 Chronicles 7.1-3.*

The point is that true worship leads us into the presence of God, and the presence of God stirs up true worship.

This is the worship cycle.

God has a never-ending stream of glory to inspire us into fresh, new and true worship, and when we worship in response to His glory, we are inviting God to show us more of His glory, which will no doubt inspire us to worship Him again!

Worship never needs to get dull.

That's just unnecessary.

The redeemed people Jesus has transformed us into by His grace and power are designed to want to worship.

If we find ourselves with hearts not wanting to worship the solution is not to crack on in spite of them. The solution is to bring them to God so that He can explain our hearts to us, and so He can heal them.

Through Him ministering to us at the very centre of who we are, we will be moved to give thanks.

His activity in our hearts will lead us to want to worship.

Through worshipping we are inviting God to minister to us again.

And so the cycle continues.

It's also worth mentioning at this point that the gathered nation of Israel *all* sing the same thing in both of the above mentioned *2 Chronicles* passages. The Spirit moves the united gathered people in such a way that they *all* sing exactly the same thing at the same time![5]

---

5. We can also see another moment of corporate Spirit led activity in *(cont. on next page)*

Whilst it is important to know how we as individuals truly worship God, there is huge value in worshipping Him together as a unified body.

We are all individuals before God, but sometimes it is really good to let that fade to become aware of God's people joined together before Him.

You are one of a number, and we are a number of ones.

As we seek to be people who worship God truly, both in the individual and cooperate sense, let us know that we do not need to *force* ourselves to worship, but that we get to *allow* ourselves to worship.

My Break

For a period of my life I lived trying to force myself to worship regardless of my feelings. Most Sundays I would make myself sing loudly and raise my hands into the air, believing that this was what choosing to worship was all about.

As I lived in this fashion, I didn't tend to my own heart. I don't think I even knew how my heart was doing!

After a time, all the things I hadn't attended to broke out and broke me apart.

You see, my heart wanted to talk to Jesus so that it could become whole again, but I thought that all of the emotions and desires within it needed to be suppressed and avoided in order to worship God well.

But I needn't have been afraid or ashamed of my feelings.

Acts 4.23-26, when the gathered believers in Jerusalem all pray the same thing at the same time.

Often when our hearts are communicating negative things, we are ashamed of them and try to silence them, not realising that our hearts could be wanting to invite God into the very emotions we are tying to silence!

I just needed to listen and give my heart permission to speak.

Not permission to rule me, but permission to be heard.

My personal love for sung worship comes from this time in my life. As my heart forced me to open up all of myself to God, He changed me and I had increasingly eye-opening encounters with Jesus.

The vast majority of these happened during times of worship, public and private.

As I allowed my heart to truly feel all it was feeling, without me trying to squash it, the choice to worship changed for me.

Instead of my choice being to sing out as loudly as I could, and raise my hands when I didn't want to, the choice became to bring my heart to the fore and allow God to speak to me.

And when He spoke, it resulted in me wanting to worship.

Just like in the chapter *Humble Pie*, where we saw how humility is a natural response to being soft-hearted in God's presence, so it is worship!

When we are totally ourselves with God, soft-hearted before Him, it allows Him to show more of Himself to us.

Not that He isn't totally Himself without us, but because He loves us partnering with Him, He often waits for us to be honest with Him before He reveals more of Himself to us.

He doesn't entrust Himself to those who aren't willing to entrust themselves to Him.

When I open myself up to God with how I am, I am being true to myself, but also to Him.

I am trusting Him with me.

I'm choosing to open up to Him, to come out of hiding and stand stripped back before Him.

And that choice is the true cost of worship; to come out of hiding, into God's presence.

A Needed Change

At my last church I had the opportunity to lead services and times of sung worship.

I had correctly known that it is a leader's privilege to model what it means to choose to worship. However, because of what God was doing in my life, my understanding of what it meant to 'choose to worship' had changed.

In times of sung worship, church leaders do have a responsibility to set a good atmosphere and expectation for the people they lead.

But the question we must ask is;

"How do leaders best fulfil that responsibility?"

Is it by forcing themselves to be the picture of a passionate worshipper, regardless of whether genuine desire is actually there in that instant?

Or is it by coming before God with all of themselves, opening themselves up, including all of their emotions, trusting that God will meet with them and create explosive worship within them?

The truth is that the greatest impact leaders can have on the people they lead, is to be ignited by a genuine desire and passion for Jesus that is fuelled by encounters with the person of Jesus.

We can only love Him because He loves us, and so we can only express our love to Him because He expresses His love to us.

Instead of taking shortcuts in worship under the guise of 'choosing to worship', perhaps we can open ourselves up to God, allowing Him to speak into our emotions and feelings, no matter what they are.

We've become good at explaining why worship is important, but perhaps we need to spend more time understanding how we can worship well?

I suggest we stop teaching people how to force themselves to worship no matter how they are feeling, and start helping people to come out of hiding, opening their hearts to God, allowing Him to transform and change them, so they can actually be free to express worship wholly, with all of themselves.

Return To Trust

I wonder whether, unconsciously and unwittingly, we may have stopped trusting the Holy Spirit to lead us into true worship.

We see the impact that worship can have on people, or more accurately, the impact that God can have on people during times of worship, and so can seek to push people into encountering God in a context of worship.

A healthy Christian leader's greatest desire is to see people transformed by the power of the person of Jesus.

But in my limited experience as a leader in a church context, I sometimes tried to force people into passion and an encounter with God, instead of letting the Spirit lead them there. I would lay challenges and targets for individuals to achieve in their day-to-day walks with God in an attempt to stir within them some sort of zeal for the Father.

I didn't let the Spirit lead me in helping others grow in their love for Him. I took it upon myself to stir and create passion within them through the challenges and targets I set them.

But all I achieved through my self-initiated challenges and target setting was to build walls between the people I was leading and Jesus.

Unknowingly, I was ingraining within them the belief that they had to *do* certain things in order to truly reach Jesus.

We can so want people to become passionate about Jesus that we hinder them actually doing it.

Ultimately, if someone does not have a deep fire burning within them for Jesus, then the Holy Spirit is the only one who can truly, genuinely alter that.

We can confront a person's apathy, we can challenge them in their faith or we can set spiritual targets for them, but if the Holy Spirit isn't leading us to do so, we're wasting our time, and possibly leading our friends astray.[6]

In reality, all we need do is create spaces for people to encounter God in whatever way the Holy Spirit chooses.

We certainly don't need to panic about it.

There will be times when the Holy Spirit asks us to confront apathy in

---

[6]. Fortunately, God has a beautiful knack of redeeming our poor intentions and using them for His purposes. Whilst this reassures us in light of mistakes we have made, we mustn't use it to justify our want to stir other people's passion ourselves.

someone around us, or requests that we help people create rhythms and disciplines that will encourage them to channel and grow in their faith.

Yet the fruitfulness of those things depends upon whether the Spirit advised and led them, not in the challenges or rhythms themselves.

As we share with others the rhythms and habits the Spirit has taught us, He may speak to them about shaping the patterns of their own life in a similar way, but He also may not.

And as we listen to others share the spiritual disciplines they practice, we get to listen for the Spirit's voice within their words to help us guide and shape our own daily practices. They may be similar, but they also may not.

The Spirit is the only one with the wisdom and methods to stir each of us into the fullness of life that is found in worshipping the person of Jesus Christ.

I don't think that teaching people that they *should, ought,* and *must* worship God enables them to come before God as they are. I believe it can set people at war with themselves, mind against heart.

That does not make whole disciples.

It makes broken, pretending ones.

So, in our leadership and friendship with those around us, what does it look like for us to trust the Holy Spirit with the passion and faith of others?

What would it take for us to place our own wisdom aside and allow the Holy Spirit to use us in leading others into true worship?

Perhaps then we will be able to instruct, guide and advise people in worship, not according to our own perceptions, but according to the wisdom of the Spirit.

Your Sound, Your Song And Your Moves

It is important for each of us to understand that every healthy expression of love for Jesus is wholly legitimate and excellent worship.

And it is important to realise that the ability to sing, paint, dance or do whatever else to a very high standard, does not equate to 'better' worship.

It is our hearts that equate to true worship, not our ability.

Each of us has different ways of expressing our deep love for Jesus.

I know some people who are very loud, some who love to dance and some who shout.

I also know some who silently stand with tears in their eyes.

A while back, I had the privilege of praying with someone silently in our heads. I was immensely moved and felt the presence of God strongly. In that moment, that person's love for Jesus was expressed in silent prayer.

That's really, really good.

We must not use this as a licence to avoid expressing worship to God in ways we feel uncomfortable doing; but we must also be confident that our heart-felt response to Him, as long as it is genuine and not an excuse to avoid being awkward or exposed, is wholly legitimate.

We mustn't hold back from expressions of worship due to fear, control or embarrassment.

We don't need to be embarrassed of anything.

But equally, we must not be ashamed, or do ourselves down, if our worship doesn't *appear* as whole-hearted or as radical as those around us.

You know your heart.

Back yourself.

We must have true confidence in our response to God.

Even if we do find ourselves worshipping to try to look radical, or not worshipping because of a fear of what others may think, we still don't need to panic or become ashamed.

God is gentle and gracious.

Begin to work through your heart with Him and He will help you to become the worshipper only you can be.

Every true expression of loving Him is completely legitimate. Yet, if we feel like God is inviting us to worship Him in a way unfamiliar to us, we can trust Him and go for it.

He will only invite us into something that is for our good.

The Holy Spirit within us is teaching us how to worship and, due to the fact that God is endless in all of His wonders, there are countless responses in the hearts of humankind to His greatness.

Dom

My dear friend Dom led the sung worship at our wedding.

The beauty of Dom's worship leading is that he is comfortable and confident in leading worship while being true to himself and his heart.

Dom has spent a lot of time journeying with God in worship. He has taken time to discover his way of worshipping.

His sound.

It's hard to describe it beyond saying that it is Dom being wholly Dom responding to God.

The main job of someone leading times of sung worship is to create a safe space for others to worship and encounter Jesus; and this is exactly what Dom did at our wedding.

Worship leading is not developed through learning songs off by heart, or by having a stunning voice.

It is learnt in the core of one's self.

If you are a worship leader, you need to find your sound.

What are you like when God moves your heart to sing?

What is your natural, creative response to the glory of God?

What do you do when God's tangible presence enters the room?

I Don't Dance

For some of us, the invitation to discover and learn our unique way of responding to God in worship feels more threatening than exciting.

Perhaps we have become so weighed down by the 'shoulds' and 'oughts' that can so often surround worship, that we don't even want to think about it.

When we see others worshipping freely and whole-heartedly we find ourselves saying; *"I don't do that."*

The good news is that we don't have to force ourselves to discover how we worship.

Worship is an invitation, not an obligation!

King David is a wonderful example of this. He was described as a man after God's own heart[7], and He loved to worship.

In *2 Samuel 6.14,* the ark of the covenant, which is where God's presence lived at that time, is returned to Jerusalem after being stolen by one of Israel's enemies. King David is so excited at the return of God's presence that he takes his outer clothing off and dances in the streets of Jerusalem.

I don't believe David chose to dance because he thought it was needed, or because it was what he thought he ought to do; he danced because he was expressing the joy he felt at the presence of God returning to Jerusalem.

To be free to respond to God in worship isn't always easy. It doesn't always feel natural for us to lose our self-awareness and go for it, whatever that looks like for us.

Once again though, we must remind ourselves that God has our best in mind in all He does.

God knows that the way for us to experience life to the full is by giving ourselves fully to Him, allowing our affection and attention to be totally towards Him.

This is His heart.

He wants to demonstrate His marvellous character to us, which in turn draws our eyes towards Him and leads us in giving thanks to Him.

---

7. *1 Samuel 13.14.*

His acts of goodness in our lives draw us to worship.

As we worship, being truly ourselves, He ministers truly as Himself; the Him full of glory, goodness, faithfulness and enduring lovingkindness.

God is inviting us to come alive, as He made us to be, by stepping boldly and freely into a lifestyle of unshackled worship of Him.

This worship has no fixed form, no formula.

It is defined by the heart from which it is given.

A heart given wholly to God.

A pure heart.

If we don't find ourselves truly excited by the possibility of this lifestyle of worship, full of emotion, choice, desire, thoughts, intellect and every other corner of ourselves, then may I suggest that we need to see God afresh?

If there is enough glory in God to move us to worship Him for eternity, then there is surely enough glory in God to move us to worship Him here and now.

What's holding us back from that part of heaven on earth?

10. THE DYING FISH

The violent demise of the defeated

A Note Before We Begin

I am all too aware that during this chapter I walk a very thin line between the optimism that I believe Scripture encourages around the defeated nature of Satan, and the painful reality of suffering and evil that many face every day.

The pain, anguish, death, destruction and hurt that Satan causes must not be ignored or brushed under the carpet in the name of Jesus, and yet the truth of the victory of Jesus needs to be faithfully painted and proclaimed.

As you read this chapter please will you bear with me?

I have tried to make it clear that Satan's impact on our world today is anything but minor and laughable; that we must fully engage with and acknowledge the damage he does. And yet, I am also compelled to write faithfully about what I perceive the Scriptures to say about the victory that Jesus has won over Satan and death.

With this in mind, let us begin.

Satan's Present Reality

> *And the angels who did not stay within their own position of authority, but left their proper dwelling, He[God] has kept in eternal chains under gloomy darkness until the judgment of the great day.*
> JUDE 6 ESV

Every Christian must somehow try and hold together the tension found in Scripture between the anguish caused by the evil present in our world[1], and the fact that Jesus defeated Satan at the cross,

---
1. *Luke 21.25-31.*

enabling God's kingdom to begin unfolding here on earth.[2]

It seems incongruous that God's kingdom, marked by wholeness, wellness and peace, can be increasing when persecution, war, famine and natural disasters are so rife around us.

Our world is caught in the battle between two kingdoms.

The kingdom of God, and the kingdom of Satan.

Ever since the fall of humankind in the Garden of Eden, these two kingdoms have been warring against each other.

But the entrance of Jesus marked the ultimate turning point in the war.

At no stage was God in danger of losing, but there was a definitive moment in time when Jesus entered the battle and turned it into a demonstrated victory on behalf of God the Father.

As part of Jesus' victory on the cross, we know that He ultimately defeated Satan, death and the grave.[3]

He descended to the realm of the dead, broke open the gates of hell and returned to the land of the living, before ascending to sit on His throne in the heavenly realm.

As the author of the book of *Hebrews* puts it:

> *He is the radiance of the glory of God and the exact imprint of His nature, and He upholds the universe by the word of His power. After making purification for sins, He sat down at the right hand of the Majesty on high.*
> HEBREWS 1.3 ESV

---

2. *Isaiah 9.7.*

3. *2 Timothy 1.10.*

Jesus accomplished the cleansing of all our sin and fulfilled the debt we owed to God the Father.[4]

And once He had done all of that, He sat down at the right hand of the Father.

And this is where He is now: sitting down!

You only sit down when you're done; when you've completed and finished all that you set out to do.

In terms of the work that Jesus did whilst on earth, He fulfilled *everything* that was in God the Father's heart and mind for Him to do.

And one of the amazing things God achieved through Jesus' life and death on earth, was the defeat of the the Devil—Jesus is the serpent crusher.[5]

And a serpent doesn't live long with a crushed head.

Casting our minds back to the verse from *Jude* at the beginning of this chapter, we can see that the *current* state of the disobedient angels, the chief of whom is Satan, is that they are being *"kept in eternal chains under gloomy darkness".*

Through Jesus' death and resurrection, He defeated Satan and has him bound in chains to be eternally destroyed on Jesus' return.

Satan is bound.

He exists in a defeated state.

When Jesus returns He will complete the destruction of Satan, but,

---

4. *1 Peter 3.18.*

5. *Genesis 3.15 & Psalm 91.13.*

according to Scripture, in the meantime Satan is in chains, in gloomy darkness; pinned under Jesus' heel.

This is Satan's present reality.

A bound prisoner awaiting final judgement.

No Thing Left To Do

Then comes the end, when He delivers the kingdom to God the Father after destroying every rule and every authority and power.

For He must reign until He has put all His enemies under His feet.

The last enemy to be destroyed is death."
1 CORINTHIANS 15.24-26 ESV

Paul understood that the victory of Jesus was total.

In *1 Corinthians 15.24-26*, Paul is explaining to his readers the events preceding the return of Christ.

In a nutshell, Paul claims that Jesus will return and hand the kingdom over to His Father after *"destroying every rule and every authority and power"*.

And, according to Paul, *"the last enemy to be destroyed is death"*.

This means that once death is defeated, there is no thing left to do and no power that still needs overthrowing, before Jesus can return and hand the kingdom over to the Father.

In Paul's second letter to Timothy, Paul says plain as day, that death has already been defeated:

> *Christ Jesus, who has destroyed death and has brought life and immortality to light through the gospel.*
> 2 TIMOTHY 1.10 NIV

Paul uses the past tense in this letter because he is referring to something that has *already* happened!

Death *has* been defeated.

Yes, death is still present in our world, but Scripture tells us that Jesus has already defeated it.

The only possible conclusion available in light of these two scriptures then, is that Jesus does not need to win any further victory prior to His return.

Either He won or He didn't.

And He did.

Yes, Jesus' victory over Satan will reach its fulfilment when He returns, and it is true that Satan still lives and causes great distress and evil presently; but it also remains true that Jesus has stripped Satan of his power and bound him in chains to be eternally destroyed when He returns.

We can often doubt that Jesus has won the victory over Satan because we do not feel like we are experiencing that victory in our own lives or seeing it in the lives of those around us.

Yet the remedy to not seeing Jesus' victory in our own lives, is not to doubt whether He has won the victory; instead, the solution is to realise that Jesus is calling us ever deeper *into* His victory.

His victory over Satan is total and He is working with us, through His Spirit, to help us increasingly experience His victory in our lives and in the lives of those around us.

Similarly to what I have said in previous chapters, being victorious through Christ is not a static state, but an ever-unfolding reality.

We have been made victorious in Christ, and yet He is continually bringing us deeper into that victory.

Paul gives no wriggle room to suggest that Jesus has not achieved an absolute win.

But if we were in any doubt, he clears it up for us in *Colossians 2.15*:

> *And having disarmed the powers and authorities, He made a public spectacle of them, triumphing over them by the cross.*
> COLOSSIANS 2.15 NIV

Paul tells the church in Colossae that once Jesus had stripped, or *"disarmed"*, Satan and the other ministers of evil, *"the powers and authorities"*, He pulled back the curtain so that the world could see their defeated nature; *"He made a public spectacle of them, triumphing over them by the cross"*.

Once Jesus had triumphed over the powers and authorities, He was raised from the dead, ascended into Heaven and then sat down.

He sat down because He had done it all.

The last power is overthrown and defeated.

That's a fact.

Our Present Reality

Now of course, *1 Corinthians 15* tells us that once Jesus has defeated death, He will return and hand the kingdom over to the Father.

But this has not yet happened.

Jesus has not returned, nor has He handed the kingdom over to the Father.

We can draw one of two conclusions from this.

The first conclusion could be that death has not yet been defeated, because if it had been, Jesus would have returned.

Fortunately, however, as we've just seen, Scripture doesn't allow this conclusion any room within its pages.

Scripture explicitly tells us both that death has been dealt with and that death will become a thing of the past when Jesus returns.

This leaves us with the second conclusion; that we exist in the time between the defeat of death, and the return of Jesus.

Just because Jesus hasn't returned yet does not mean that He didn't defeat death; it just means that the Father doesn't deem this point in time to be the right one for His Son to return.[6]

We can trust that the Father will bring about Jesus' return at the perfect time as it is a decision made from His perfection.

We live in the time between the defeat of Satan, and the demise of Satan.

But what of the warnings that Jesus gave about the strife of the end times? They don't seem to fit with the scriptures I have quoted so far that speak of Satan's defeat at the hands of Jesus:

> *'And when you hear of wars and tumults, do not be terrified,*

---

[6]. Of course, we must remember that Jesus could return at any minute, like a thief in the night (*1 Peter 3.10*). Just because He has not returned, does not mean He is far off. He could return in a minute's time, or in many years.

for these things must first take place, but the end will not be at once.'

Then he said to them, 'Nation will rise against nation, and kingdom against kingdom.

There will be great earthquakes, and in various places famines and pestilences. And there will be terrors and great signs from heaven.'
LUKE 21.9-11 ESV

This passage seems to completely oppose everything I've said so far.

Jesus' victory over Satan seems to be contradicted by the story of the world around us, where pain, death and evil seems all too prevalent.

Can Satan really be bound, defeated and all authority given to us, when such destruction is our earthly reality?

How can they possibly exist hand in hand?

How can both be true?

The Dying Fish

To the title—*The Dying Fish*.

Picture the scene:

There's a drought and a river has almost entirely dried up.

A few fish have been caught out and are left in little pools of water, which are quickly vanishing in the midday sun.

The more the water around the fish evaporates, the more violently they flap and squirm in the futile hope that they might find some hidden pool of water to save them.

When fish are taken out of water, they thrash about terribl
to fling themselves back into water.

As the puddle a fish is in shrinks, so the thrashing of the fish increases.

I think that Satan is like this at the moment.

Like a dying fish.

His environment is shrinking fast.

Jesus is conquering Satan's domain steadily, and the definitive demise of Satan's kingdom is wholly guaranteed by Jesus' death and resurrection.

Currently, pockets of Satan's domain are being re-taken by God's people living into the authority God has given them to establish the kingdom of Heaven on earth here and now!

And the more that Satan's domain shrinks, the more violent he gets.

This is why it can be easy to believe that Satan is growing in influence and power.

Please understand that Satan's violence is all too real. Just because his domain is shrinking does not mean that he is not causing immense pain, strife, fear and hurt. Satan is still trying to destroy everything God longs to preserve and redeem.

Satan is desperately fighting his bonds and prison to try and steal back all that Jesus is reclaiming in the world.

In the moments before the final return of Jesus, Satan will be at his most violent. He will be causing the most pain, the most hurt and the most distress.

But this need not pull us down.

Think of a fly before and after being sprayed with fly spray.

The moment before you spray it, the fly is completely calm and often still.

However, as soon as it is sprayed and begins to die, it becomes incredibly active.

If we didn't know better, we might think that the spray had invigorated the fly with a new zeal for life.

Yet we know that is not what is truly happening.

The moment Jesus died on the cross, Satan's fate was sealed.

There is no other possible outcome for Satan other than eternal death.

From that eternal perspective, Satan's present struggles and violence have no bearing on the outcome.

He is bound and when Jesus returns, He will be destroyed.

But until Jesus returns, Satan will be stirring one hell of a fuss, making increasingly desperate, but intensely painful and destructive swings, in a vain attempt to try and stop the inevitable victory of Jesus and His people.

So, as we are faced with the reality of Satan's activity in our world, let us heed the words of Jesus from *Luke 21*:

> *Now when these things begin to take place, straighten up and raise your heads, because your redemption is drawing near.*
> LUKE 21.28 ESV

> *So also, when you see these things taking place, you know that the kingdom of God is near.*
> LUKE 21.31 ESV

More Real Than Real

In *Luke 21.28* Jesus encourages His disciples to lift their heads when they are confronted with great evil and anguish in the last days.

Lift their heads because there is another story.

In the spiritual realm, Jesus is sitting on His throne, having achieved all He was sent to achieve on earth, and Satan is imprisoned, awaiting the judgement that will befall him when Jesus returns.

Jesus is the name above every other name[7], God the Father has placed all things under His feet[8], and He has rendered heaven's greatest enemy powerless.[9]

What is more, we have been elevated to sit with Him, in the place where everything is under His feet.[10]

This is the reality of the spiritual realm.

It is not a dream, nor a future hope; it is a present reality.

When Jesus returns, the physical and the spiritual will become one again.

God will recreate the dwelling place of humankind, making it one

---

7. *Philippians 2.9.*
8. *Ephesians 1.22.*
9. *Hebrews 2.14b.*
10. *Ephesians 2.4-6.*

with His dwelling place.

Jesus calls His disciples to raise their heads in *Luke 21.28* because the reality of the spiritual realm is the reality that the physical realm is heading towards.

Not the other way round.

The perfection of heaven is unfolding on earth.

The brokenness of earth is not unfolding in heaven.

So let us not be disheartened by evil. Let us look heavenwards and remind ourselves of the reality in the spiritual realm. The reality that is ever becoming our reality here, and will one day become the perfect reality of the new creation.

That's A Big Fish

I want to be very careful to leave no room to be misunderstood; I am not suggesting that Satan's impact in the world today is minimal or laughable.

Every one of us has encountered evil in our lives.

The pain and anguish caused by Satan's activity is devastating beyond what is possible to express in words.

Satan causes pain because it is who he is and what he does.

Evil is present and it wants to destroy and hurt every person alive; to deceive us that God is not good, and that God is not able.

Satan may be dying, bound and doomed, but he is still very big.

He's a huge fish.

As he thrashes around in response to Jesus' victory, Satan is capable of doing a lot of damage.

Please do not think that a victorious mindset means being unrealistic.

We must fully feel and acknowledge the pain and strife caused by Satan so that we can be a part of seeing that pain and strife overcome by the blood of Jesus.

In order to bring light into darkness, we must realise that there is darkness around us.

It is only when we are in the darkest places that we have the privilege of bringing in the light of Christ.

It is a challenging road to walk—to live in the victory of Jesus, fully expecting good to occur as His kingdom unfolds, yet at the same time to not disconnect from, or deny, the destructive, evil impact Satan is having on people we love, and the world around us.

In order to engage fully in bringing the light of Jesus into dark places, we must understand both Jesus' victory, and Satan's tactics.

So, having talked about the nature of Jesus' victory already, let us now look at some of Satan's tactics so that we are better equipped for our heavenly mandate.

Hell's Arsenal

In *John 10.10* and *John 8.44*, Jesus names four weapons that Satan uses against humankind:

Lying, stealing, killing and destroying.

These weapons all damage what God created to be good and perfect.

Killing and destroying are the methods Satan uses to extinguish life, stealing is how he robs us of the truth, and lying is the way in which he twists God's truth.

I would like to focus specifically on Satan's weapon of lying, because it is often the subtlest and most difficult weapon to identify, at the same time as being the most prominent weapon linked to Satan himself – the father of lies.[11]

The lies the Devil sows are always twisted truths.

Satan's lies always distort, deceive and misrepresent truth.

Distortion is the act of twisting and manipulating truth, deception is tricking someone into believing a truth is not what it seems, and misrepresentation is making a truth from God appear to be bad by warping who we believe God to be.

We can see examples of Satan's lies in *Luke 4*, when he is tempting Jesus in the wilderness.

In the first temptation, Satan tried to trick Jesus into believing that the most important hunger in His life was physical hunger, not spiritual hunger.

It is true that hunger is essential, but spiritual hunger is always more important than physical hunger.

The power that Jesus had was not first and foremost to meet the needs of His body, it was to serve the Father.

The food He truly craved was doing His Father's will.[12]

---

11. *John 8.44.*
12. *John 4.34.*

So Jesus took the truth the Devil had lied about, untwisted it and declared it back to the Devil as a rebuke, saying:

> *It is written, 'Man shall not live by bread alone.'*
> LUKE 4.4 ESV

In the second temptation the lie was: worship the Devil and you'll get authority.

No! Jesus already has authority and He is committed to serving God with His God-given authority!

The Devil tries to convince Jesus that He needs to rebel against God in order to get something God has already given Him.

Yet Jesus holds firm and says:

> *'You shall worship the Lord your God,*
> *and Him only shall you serve.'*
> LUKE 4.8 ESV

Finally, Satan asks Jesus to prove that God would protect Him by jumping off a building, so that God would send angels to catch Him before He dashed even a toe on the stones below.[13]

The Devil was telling Jesus that God's protection needed to be tested to be trusted.

But Jesus wasn't having any of it:

> *It is said, 'You shall not put the Lord your God to the test.'*
> LUKE 4.9-11 ESV

Each time the Devil twisted a truth, tried to deceive Him, or tried to

---

13. *Luke 4.9-11.*

misrepresent God in Jesus' mind, Jesus' response was to identify the lie and to remedy it with the truth.

We can also see Satan's lies in the story of Adam and Eve.[14]

In the book of *Genesis*, the Devil lied to Adam and Eve by convincing them that God was impinging on their freedom by asking them to not eat from the tree of the knowledge of good and evil, when originally God asked them not to eat from that tree to ensure their freedom.

Satan tricked Adam and Eve into believing that God was against them and imprisoning them, which led Adam and Eve to mistrust Him.

If that isn't misrepresentation, I don't know what is.

Unfortunately, unlike Jesus, Adam and Eve believed Satan's lie because they didn't hold onto the truth that would expose the lie for what it was.

So how can we respond to Satan's lies like Jesus did and not believe them, like Adam and Eve?

Our Response

Jesus' response to Satan's lies should inspire us all.

Instead of burying our heads in the sand when Satan lies to us, we can look the lie boldly in the face, knowing that the Spirit will lead us in rebuking it.

As the kingdom of God advances, it inevitably comes up against the shrinking kingdom of darkness. Facing the father of lies is a sure sign that we are furthering God's kingdom!

---

14. *Genesis 3.1-7.*

As God's kingdom unfolds, we see insights and receive revelations of God.

The more truth we see of God, the more material the Devil has to twist into lies.

This is because every time God reveals a new truth to us, Satan has a new truth to distort.

However, every moment we spend with God equips us to be able to better discern what is coming from Him, and what is coming from Satan.

The more time we spend in the light, the easier it is to recognise darkness.

> *When He has brought out all His own, He goes before them, and the sheep follow Him, for they know His voice.*
>
> *A stranger they will not follow, but they will flee from Him, for they do not know the voice of strangers.*
> JOHN 10.4-5 ESV

Just before Jesus tells His disciples that Satan has come to steal, kill and destroy, He explains that He is the Shepherd and that those who follow Him are His sheep. What's more, His sheep know His voice and flee any other voice.

In essence, Jesus is saying that the best way to break free from, and not trip over Satan's lies, is to be very close to the Shepherd; not because being close to the Shepherd means that we don't hear the lies of the thief, but because by being close to the Shepherd we will instinctively flee the voice of the thief because we'll know that it isn't the voice of Jesus.

We'll know the difference.

lies from Satan is to be expected because Satan is a liar.

There can be the days where we feel ashamed that Satan is trying to speak to us!

It is true that sometimes we have opened ourselves up to hearing a lie through an unwise decision; but the Holy Spirit will let us know if this is the case, and we can repent and move on.

Most of the time, however, Satan's lies aren't down to us doing something wrong, it is just him being who he is.

A liar.

With the Spirit guiding us, we can now take any lie that Satan speaks over us and redeem it.

If a lie is a twisted truth then surely it can be untwisted.

We can redeem the lie.

Take the example of comparison; looking at someone else and their gifting, and measuring ourselves either less or more favourably against them.

We begin to derive our sense of worth from whether we think we are better or worse than those around us.

When I have found myself struggling with comparison, I have come to understand that there is one underlying belief underpinning it all; that I am only valuable if I'm the best.

If we believe this lie and act upon it, we will, in our hearts, end up begrudging those we think are better than us, and looking down on those we consider to be less than us. We'll struggle with an insatiable, unhealthy competitiveness, and be critical and judgemental of others in an attempt to put ourselves above them in our own estimations.

The truth with which to replace this lie is that I'm valued *regardless* of my talent and ability.

It is right to try to be the best that I can be with the gifts that God has given to me, but in *response* to the value God places on me.

Can you see the way Satan twisted it?

He took the truth that we are all made valuable in God's sight, and twisted it so that I thought I had to obtain value in God's sight through my ability to outshine others.

Untwisting the truth enabled me to see that I am *already* valued by God, and that nothing I do can increase or decrease His valuation of me. The same truth tells me I am no more nor less valuable than anyone else.

If I become free from the lie, comparison can be replaced with celebration!

Instead of deriving my worth from whether my ability stacks up favourably against other people, I find freedom to celebrate others when they excel.

You see, we are made to notice the strengths and weaknesses of those around us. Not so that we feel in awe of them, or inferior to them, but so that we can celebrate other people's skills, and help each other to grow in our areas of weakness.

Another benefit of being freed from comparison is that it enables us to be open-handed with the gifts God has given us.

If our worth comes from whether we are better at certain things than others, we would never want to impart what gifts we have to anyone else! We wouldn't want to train people or give them advice.

What a dull and tight-fisted community we would have if we didn't have open-handed spiritual mothers and fathers!

There is so much to be gained through not being fearful of Satan. Yet ironically, one of his biggest lies is that we should be scared of him!

Yes, we need to be aware of his schemes and tactics, but not so that we can cower in hiding, but so that we can confront Satan and be a part of his demise.

I'm not encouraging us to spend lots of time *trying* to hear Satan lie, but given that he is going to whisper lies to us, it is good to know what to do with them, and how to redeem what he says.

How powerless does it render the Devil if even what he says can bring us straight to God?

When put next to the power and authority of Jesus, Satan's lies need hold no power over us.

No power whatsoever.

The authority Satan wanted so badly, that He tried to seize through war with God, has been given to God's people as a free gift.

What Satan was unable to steal through rebellion, we have been given through relationship.

The authority of God is a gift to be received, not a right to be seized.

It is time for us to see that everything is redeemable.

Nothing is lost.

God is unrelenting in His redemptive nature.

Everything that was lost can be won back.

We can be exceedingly hopeful about every area of our lives.

Will you join hands with God in your heart, mind and life, to see the redemptive truths of God untwist every distortion, deception and misrepresentation the Devil has thrown and will throw your way?

Considering The Eternal

But not a hair on your heads shall perish. By your steadfastness and patient endurance you shall win the true life of your souls.
LUKE 21.18-19 AMP

As we've seen earlier on in this chapter, the desperate flailing of Satan can seriously damage and hurt us.

The good news is that the Holy Spirit is always present and ready to instruct us in how to use the heavenly authority Jesus has made available to us to defeat the Devil's schemes in our personal lives.

Whether it be the greatest stronghold, or a seemingly small lie, we can stand firm in the knowledge that God has won.

Our freedom is a certainty in eternity, and God is inviting us to taste it now.

We need not pretend that the lies of Satan do no affect us, or those around us.

We are called to be honest people, wholly empathetic towards those who suffer at his hands.

We are to weep with those who weep.

However, gone are the days when affliction in the world and in our lives should leave us with fear.

Now it should leave us with at least these two things: Hope and resolve. Hope, because Jesus has won and that fact is now woven into the very fabric of the earth, and everything on the earth. He is seated with His Father in the knowledge that victory is already guaranteed.

Hope grows within us as we engage in a battle where the outcome is already determined, against an enemy who is chained and doomed, albeit flailing until the last.

And secondly, resolve, because even though it may appear that the Devil is wreaking more and more damage in our world, we have been given a higher perspective that tells us otherwise.

We have the truth to disarm Satan's lies, and we have a love that triumphs over fear.

We see that we have what Satan always wanted, heaven's authority, and we get to speed his ultimate destruction by living lives infused with delight, faith and confidence in the person of Jesus.

Every moment we spend in delight and awe of Jesus we shrink what little remains of the Devil's kingdom that bit more.

Resolve to feel the pain of others, without letting despair marry sympathy, which it so often does.

Resolve to cry with others experiencing pain, at the same time holding fast to faith and hope, cloaked in love.

Death cannot hold us.

So what is there left to fear?

Surely not a dying fish.

11. IS IT HARD?

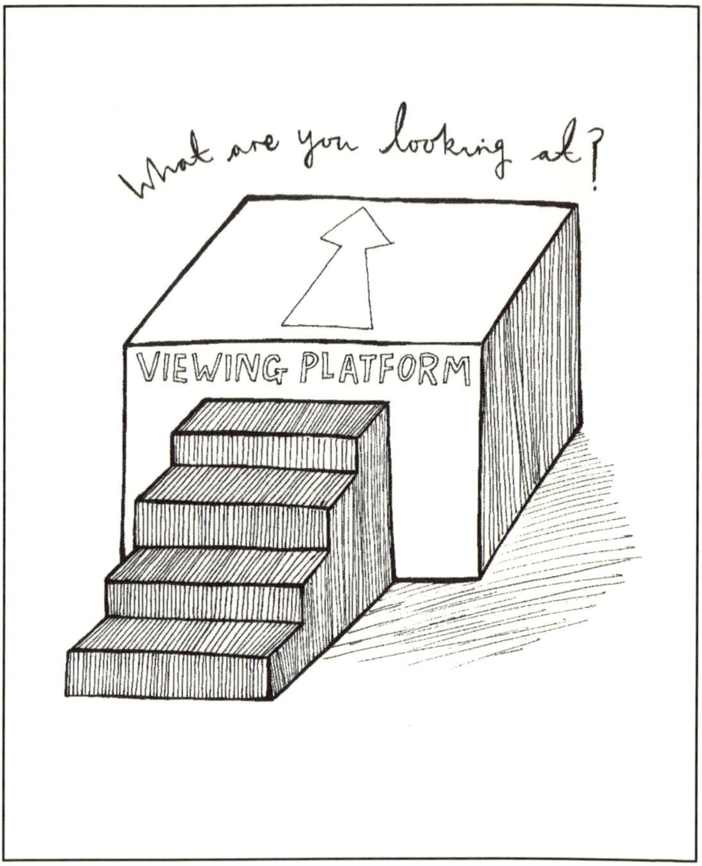
What are you looking at?
VIEWING PLATFORM

A Party Question

Someone once took me aside during a Christmas party and asked me whether I found being a Christian hard.

Now, apart from the fact that I was taken slightly off guard at being asked this at a Christmas party, I really enjoyed thinking about this question.

My answer at the time was average at best, but the question has stayed with me; what did they mean when they asked, *"Is it hard?"*

If they had asked whether the Christian life has hardships, the answer would be simple.

Undoubtedly, the Christian walk has hardships.

It is death to self to give one's life into the hands of Jesus, trusting Him in all eventualities, which will include persecution, just as Scripture warned.[1]

That sounds hard.

But that wasn't quite the question, was it?

I was asked whether I consider being a Christian hard, not whether I thought the Christian walk contains hardships. The difference, albeit subtle, is important; one requires a factual 'yes' or 'no', the other is asking for an opinion.

---

1. *2 Timothy 3.12.*

Super Alex

Infuriatingly, a few months ago my friend Alex managed to complete a quadrathlon having done next to no training.[2]

The quadrathlon is a gruelling endurance event involving long distance swimming, cycling, kayaking and running, one after the other.

If I were to even consider the prospect of doing a quadrathlon myself, my mind would let me know in no uncertain terms that it is not something I want to do. The prospect of the pain, pulled muscles and all manner of other injuries, would help steer me well clear of the whole thing!

As a rule of thumb, we don't tend to choose to put ourselves through painful situations unless there is a gain greater than the pain.

Alex did not compete in the quadrathlon for the pain he knew it would cause him.

Alex competed to be alongside his brother, to have the elation of finishing and the satisfaction of pushing his body to its limit.

He chose to compete because of all the positives he saw, and in the build up, he actually looked forward to it!

There were aspects of doing the quadrathlon that excited him and made the pain it caused bearable.

When I ask Alex about the quadrathlon, his overriding memory is one of enjoyment and satisfaction. Even though the race undoubtedly had challenges, trials and painful moments, Alex doesn't remember the race primarily by them.

---

2. I know, he's just one of those people.

The Abandoned Lover

In the book of the Bible, *Song of Songs*, there is a story of a man and woman's romantic relationship.

It is quite the dramatic tale.

In the middle of the story, just after the young lovers have married, the man comes to where his wife is sleeping and knocks on the door, asking to come in. She feels very tired and has already gone through the effort of getting ready for bed, so doesn't want to get up to open the door to him.[3]

Eventually, she remembers how much she adores her husband, and so gets up to let him in. Unfortunately for her, he is now no longer there, and she says:

> *I opened for my beloved,*
> *but my beloved had left; he was gone.*
> *My heart sank at his departure.*
> *I looked for him but did not find him.*
> *I called him but he did not answer.*
>
> *The watchmen found me*
> *as they made their rounds in the city.*
> *They beat me, they bruised me;*
> *they took away my cloak,*
> *those watchmen of the walls!*
> SONG OF SONGS 5.6-7 NIV

Not only has her husband left her, but she is then beaten, bruised and stripped of her cloak whilst searching for him. Then she finds her friends and asks them to tell her husband that she is looking for him.

---

3. *Song of Songs* 5.2-6.

But they mock her:

> *How is your beloved better than others,*
> *most beautiful of women?*
> *How is your beloved better than others,*
> *that you so charge us?*
> SONG OF SONGS 5.9 NIV

Standing in front of her mocking friends, abandoned by the man she loves, beaten and bruised by the people employed to protect the city she lives in, the woman of *Song of Songs* has to give an answer to the question;

"What is so good about this man?"

Given what she has just been through, I think that she would be justified in giving a slightly less than complimentary answer about her husband.

Perhaps she would tell her friends that he got home late, demanding to be let in, only to abandon her at the door! That she had to come out at night to look for him because, at the end of the day, he *is* her husband and she has a duty to find him... Oh the cost of being a wife!

At this her friends would all roll their eyes, chuckle in agreement and tell her that they would let her husband know that she was looking for him, bruised, beaten and somewhat unimpressed at his recent behaviour.

Not the answer she gives though:

> *My beloved is radiant and ruddy,*
> *outstanding among ten thousand.*
>
> *His head is purest gold;*
> *his hair is wavy*
> *and black as a raven.*

*His eyes are like doves
by the water streams,
washed in milk,
mounted like jewels.*

*His cheeks are like beds of spice
yielding perfume.
His lips are like lilies
dripping with myrrh.*

*His arms are rods of gold
set with topaz.
His body is like polished ivory
decorated with lapis lazuli.*

*His legs are pillars of marble
set on bases of pure gold.
His appearance is like Lebanon,
choice as its cedars.*

*His mouth is sweetness itself;
he is altogether lovely.
This is my beloved, this is my friend,
daughters of Jerusalem.*
SONG OF SONGS 5.10-16 NIV

Apart from the fact that her answer silences her mocking friends, the description of her husband is simply stunning.

You can almost feel the passion in her words, rising to her final statement, spoken with confidence and ultimate defiance:

*His mouth is sweetness itself;
he is altogether lovely.
This is my beloved, this is my friend,
daughters of Jerusalem.*
SONG OF SONGS 5.16 NIV

You see, this woman's love for her husband meant that even in a moment of intense hardship, she dwelt not on the pain, but on the glory of the one she loved.

It wasn't just a calculated, intentional choice; it was her heart's reaction to the situation in which she found herself.

She didn't have time to choose how to react; her love and passion just took her suddenly.

In fact, the woman's heart was so consumed with desire for her husband that, even in an intense moment of pain, disappointment and shame, she was still led by that desire and not by her disappointment.

All the negative emotions she might justifiably have felt completely melted away in the face of the love she had, and felt, for him.

She did not allow surrounding hardships to dim her love, even though her husband appeared to have abandoned her.

If I asked this woman whether she had found it 'hard' to love this man, I imagine she would have told me that she didn't care how hard it was.

She was in love with him and she wanted to find him.

She would have told me that she would have moved hell and high water to get him back.

She had the light of her heart to find.

When I am asked whether I find it hard being a Christian, I want to be like this woman.

I want to be so consumed with the wonders of the person of Jesus that any consideration of whether my life has been made 'hard' through following Him dissolves away to nothing.

Not so that I deny or hide from pain and hardships, but so that I ⸺ the magnificence of Jesus to dwarf them.

He does not scorn the things we find hard; He enters into them to minster to us in the midst of them.

It is so easy to swing between two extremes; either denying that we hurt, or allowing our hurts to become our primary focus.

Neither is the fullness of life promised by Jesus.

Paul suffered a great number of the hardships Jesus warned would affect His followers. Stoned, beaten, imprisoned and left for dead, he experienced a very real and drastic level of persecution for his faith.

Yet these hardships did not dominate Paul. In fact, he writes the following of those experiences:

> *Yes, furthermore, I count everything as loss compared to the possession of the priceless privilege (the overwhelming preciousness, the surpassing worth, and supreme advantage) of knowing Christ Jesus my Lord and of progressively becoming more deeply and intimately acquainted with Him [of perceiving and recognizing and understanding Him more fully and clearly].*
> PHILIPPIANS 3.8 AMP

Paul was so moved, captivated and enthralled with the person of Jesus that everything else, hardship or blessing, held little weight in comparison with his deepening, active and real relationship with Jesus Christ.

That is how he went through being beaten, stoned and imprisoned, and came out the other side with his faith and love intact.

Just as I am told that often a woman's pain in childbirth is far outweighed by the delight of holding her newborn, so Christians

ships, considering them loss in comparison to the preciousness of being in relationship with God.

Now Let Me Be Crystal

We cannot try to pretend that the hardships of life don't cause immense distress, anguish and pain.

That would be denial.

Hardships are all too real.

It would be beyond patronising and rude of me to suggest that it is easy to smile in the face of hardships simply by gazing towards God in perpetual, serene happiness.

Here in the UK, the majority of us haven't seen anything like the suffering of other Christians, and indeed people of other faiths, or no faith, across the globe and throughout the centuries.

As I have previously stressed in *The Dying Fish*, it isn't godly to try to bury pain; it is foolish.

God does not want us to ignore the sadness within us caused by suffering. He does not want us to chastise ourselves for not feeling that our hardships don't matter in comparison with knowing Him.

Considering hardships or blessings as loss in comparison to knowing Jesus is not an obligation we must strive to feel; it happens naturally as we see more of the worth of Jesus, not as we try to force ourselves to consider less of our pain.

As we see Jesus more, we become more aware of how wonderful He is and it results in all other aspects of our life carrying less and less weight for us. Not so we become negligent, but so that we grow in valuing Jesus Christ appropriately.

As we increasingly see how much He is worth, we cannot help but to realise how little everything else is worth by comparison.

The point is not to try to avoid feeling the pain of hardship; the point is how to navigate through hardship well.

How do we travel through the valley of the shadow of death until we find ourselves on the other side; on the mountains of the light of life?

As we come to God in our hardships, He reaches in, full of sympathy and kindness[4], and leads us through the pain and sadness, holding us tightly to Himself, until He has safely planted us in the land beyond the pain.[5]

Tears, anger, fear, doubt, hurt and disappointment will all be a part of our journey through life.

Hardships will be present in every life, because, as I emphasised in the previous chapter, Satan is dying, but not yet dead.

Up until the moment that Jesus returns, Satan will be causing pain and hurt with every word he speaks and every action he does. It is just who he is.

We cannot choose a life without hardships.

They are a fact of life.

People suffer truly awful things. We must never try to play them down.

---

4. *Hebrews 4.15.*

5. *Psalm 23.*

We are called to be the most sympathetic and empathetic people around.

We can approach God *in the midst of* pain. We get to be honest and emotional with Him, and to be willing to listen and respond to Him.

The more we seek God in the middle of hardships and blessings, the more He reveals of Himself to us, so the greater and more correct our perspective becomes.

So let us not deny that hardships are real, but let us fill our eyes with Jesus in spite of them, so we can come to know His far superior worth.

Let us open ourselves up to Him, in laughter and in tears, and see the comfort of the Holy Spirit walk us through darkness into light.

Jesus' Response To Hardship

Jesus is able to shepherd us through every hardship because He Himself has been there.[6]

The night that Jesus was betrayed by one of His disciples, the betrayal that led Jesus to His death, He went to pray alone. During this time, He asked God to release Him from the suffering He knew was merely hours away.[7]

And yet, He ended each prayer with the vow that He would not walk away from death if that were what God was asking of Him.

Then an angel came and strengthened Jesus.[8]

---

6. *Hebrews 2.18.*
7. *Luke 22.41-42.*
8. *Luke 22.43.*

The angel came *after* the honest prayer, not before.

The strength to face the suffering came *after* the moment of honesty, not before.

For us, dealing with hardships also requires honesty with God, and with those around us.

Sometimes God speaks to us through another person. If we avoid others in times of pain, which can be all too easy to do, we may miss out on what God has given to other people for us.[9]

This shouldn't surprise us since God chose to hide His greatest message to humankind within the form of a human.

We must also note that if someone does take the huge step to talk honestly with us about what they are going through, we get to empathise with them.

We are called to weep with those who weep and rejoice with those who rejoice.[10]

We're not always called to try and solve their problem or to give our opinion.

I believe that through our empathy, the person sharing with us can begin to see the word that God has hidden in us for them to find.

Back to Jesus though; after the angel strengthens Him, He is arrested and taken to His death. We gain a remarkable insight into Jesus' perspective on His walk to death on the cross in the book of *Hebrews*:

---

9. Not that we need to tell *everyone* about the hardships we may be enduring, but it is important to have a few others around us with whom we can share, cry and pray during our lowest moments.

10. *Romans 12.15.*

> *Who for the joy that was set before him endured the cross, despising the shame, and is seated at the right hand of the throne of God.*
> HEBREWS 12.2B ESV

The writer of *Hebrews* lets us know that Jesus was willing to go through the betrayal, pain and alienation of the cross because of the joy He saw beyond it.

He was so motivated by the prospect of the joy beyond the hardship, that He chose to go through with it, when He could have chosen not to do so.

So what was beyond the cross that filled Jesus with so much joy?[11]

His Father and fulfilling His Father's will.

Because of His delight in God, Jesus sought to do whatever God asked of Him, even dying on a cross.

Jesus knew that God's hope for humankind and the world depended on Him dying on the cross; but He did not walk the road to Jerusalem merely because of a religious duty or obligation to fulfil His Father's will. Jesus was able to endure the cross with joy, because His *delight* was in pleasing God His Father, the one He loved.

God Himself was Jesus' motivation and His joy.

His delight in pleasing God did not make the cross hurt any less.

---

11. Please note that the writer of *Hebrews* did not write, *"For the joy set before him (joy that Jesus didn't actually feel, but thought that he should feel and so pretended and told everyone that he did feel),"* Jesus actually felt joy. Not a flippant joy that cannot be present in the midst of tears and sadness, but a deep set expectation and excitement, which can be present within no matter what other emotions we are feeling.

Jesus still felt every aspect of the pain and alienation of the crucifixion.

We cannot make hardships stop hurting.

But Jesus' delight in His Father put the cross into perspective. Even when facing death, He saw something far bigger, something that excited His heart beyond it.

Jesus' delight and love of His Father gave Him the strength and perseverance to endure the suffering of the cross.

In the face of the hardest thing ever known by humankind, Jesus was still driven by joy at the prospect of closeness with His Father.

Not because He thought He *ought* to be filled with joy, but because His Father simply *was* His heart's greatest desire.

His Legacy

It is possible that our communion with God, both in its present reality and the eternal certainty, can help us to endure hardship today, just as it did with Jesus.

Think back to Alex.

He endured the quadrathlon because he knew the joy of finishing would be great, even though he would be pushing his body to its limit. In the days after the event, when he could only walk down the stairs backwards, Alex would be reminded, with a grin on his face, of the joy he felt at taking part in the race.

Our prize is God Himself, so how much greater will our joy be?

God has set His presence within us in the person of the Holy Spirit; and He didn't hold any of Himself back when He sent His Holy Spirit to live amongst us.

The fullness of God resides within us!

Not only will we have perfect access to God in eternity, we also have access to God's presence here and now all thanks to Jesus.[12]

In many senses, our eternity with God has already started, and permission to explore the endless intricacies, unending beauties and unimaginable wonders of God has already been given.

Spiritually, there is no longer any barrier between those who have their faith in Jesus, and God. Even though it sometimes feels like there is, the truth is that there is not!

Veil?

Gone.[13]

Curtain?

Torn in two.[14]

God knew that hardships would come against humankind during this interim period before Christ returns, and that is why He has come to be with us in the midst of it all. The Holy Spirit dwells in the hearts of God's people and in the fabric of all creation, leading, encouraging and loving us through any hardship or blessing, and everything else in between.

God being with us allows us to endure and prevail, not with scowls and grimaces, but with wonder and amazement that God is near.

He could not be any closer.

---

12. *Hebrews 10.19-22.*
13. *2 Corinthians 3.16 & Hebrews 10.19.*
14. *Matthew 27.51.*

It doesn't always feel like the joy of the presence of Jesus can help us to endure hardship. I certainly have moments in the midst of the slightest hardship or frustration where it doesn't feel like my heart is rejoicing at simply knowing Christ.

But that doesn't mean it isn't possible or true.

We can't always see the sun through the rain clouds.

But it's always there.

Truth isn't always obvious, but that doesn't make it any less true.

We must continually remind ourselves, and each other, about the truths and possibilities that living with faith in Christ presents. We must tell each other that God can really be *known*, and that our hearts can actually *feel* excited by Him.

Then we will be able to say that we can endure all things, because we so enjoy exploring and knowing the ever-unfolding, deep depths of the person of Jesus.

The Joyful Abandoned Lover

Remember the beaten and bruised woman from *Song of Songs*?

Even though it looked like her husband had abandoned her, she still told her friends how wonderful he was.

She was so driven by the prospect of being reunited with the one she loved that she pushed through a number of hardships to find him. She didn't think of the cost, or the pain, she thought of the joy of being with her love.

"Do you think it is hard being a Christian?"

o observe the life of a Christian from afar then perhaps I *"yes."*

I see the moments of waiting for God, the moments of uncertainty. I see the tough questions, the bracing self-honesty that the Holy Spirit invites from us, and it looks hard; not to mention the persecution that so many face every day just for professing faith in Jesus.

However, I have an insider's perspective.[15]

There are hardships, undeniably, yet I could not say that I find the Christian life hard.

If I did, I would have ceased to be more excited at the person of Jesus than I am aware of any given hardship in my life.

In comparison to Him, getting to know Him more all the time, seeing what He has done, how unrelentingly good He is, and how alive and free He makes me, it is possible for hardships to feel far less dominating.

It is right to weep and cry as we feel the pain of hardship, when evil seems close to us and those around us.

Just as Jesus wept in compassion and in anguish, so it is godly for us to do so too.[16]

Yet in the midst of the hurts we encounter, it is also possible for there to be a continually bubbling passion and excitement for the person of Jesus that holds us fast when we're shaken, leads us on when we feel at a loss, and pulls us into a tangible joy at the closeness we have with God, both now, and for all eternity.

---

15. When I say I have an insider's perspective, I mean that I'm a Christian, not that I'm one who has faced lots of hardships. Many other people have suffered far, far more than me.
16. *John 11.35* & *Luke 19.41*.

"Andrew, do you think it is hard being a Christian?"

In spite of the evil that snatches at us, in spite of the hurts that bombard us, and the tears that creep up on us, I do not consider it a hardship to follow Christ.

If Jesus can walk to the cross because of the joy set before Him, then, empowered by His Spirit within us, it is possible for us all to carry our crosses because of the joy set before us.

Not following Jesus by ignoring the pain we may feel, or walking on the other side of the road from those around us who are hurting in order to protect our 'joy', but driven by a deep love for Jesus and a desire to live as He did, we can walk through all hurts and strife with the Spirit leading and equipping us so that we maintain a sense of delight in God, no matter what we are facing.

There is a joy set before us that can far outweigh any other experience of life; a joy that can sustain us through the most challenging hardship; and that joy set before us is God Himself.

12. THE MIRROR

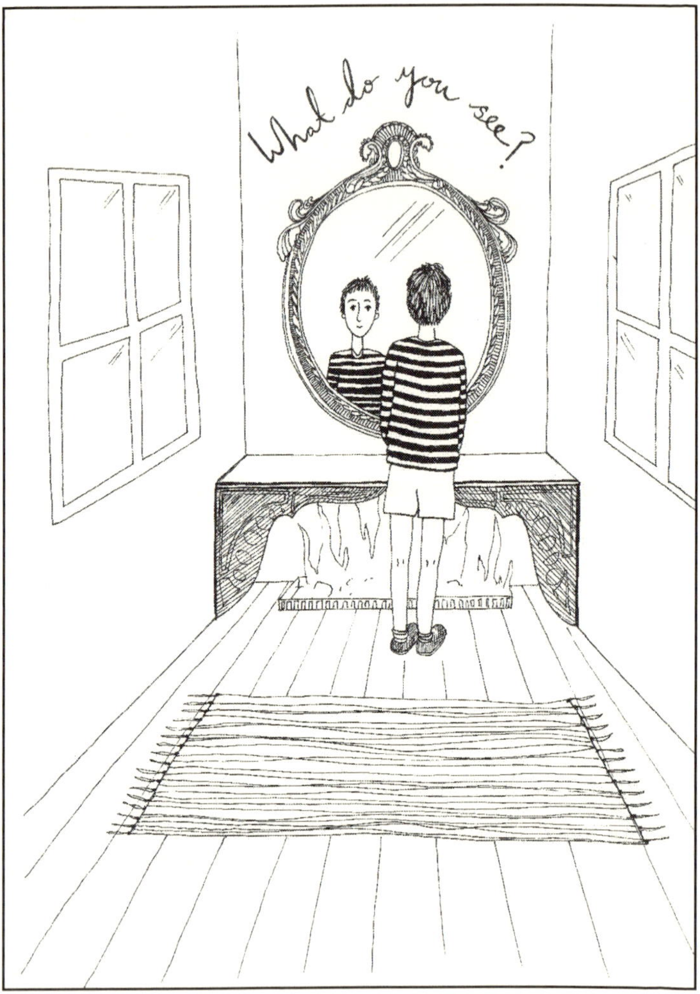
What do you see?

Which Way?

In the Disney film *Pocahontas,* there is a scene in which the heroine is in a canoe approaching a fork in a river.

The decision she must make in this moment, of which route to take down the river, symbolises a dilemma she is facing in her life. One fork of the river is wide, slow and calm, while the other plunges down a narrow, much faster gorge, filled with rapids and rocks.

After a moment's hesitation, obviously mid-song, she chooses the right-hand fork and careers towards the rapids ahead.

As this book draws to a close, I find myself wanting to ask the question;

"Which way?"

Not a lost cry that is seeking direction, but a broader question about the style of life we wish to lead as followers of Jesus.

I get the sense that what is possible in this period of history is remarkable.[1]

I believe that God wishes to do things in, through and with His people that the watching world will find incredible.

Yet perhaps many of us find ourselves, like Pocahontas, unsure of which path to take.

Our faith, our trust in Jesus, and our desire to make Him known, all remain present whichever fork we choose.

---

[1]. The option for God's people to live a more adventurous, simple and unpredictable faith, empowered and inspired by the Holy Spirit, has always been available and is not a new idea. Yet I believe that in this period of history, the choice of what kind of faith to lead is especially important and significant.

The choice we are facing is not a question between keeping faith or abandoning faith.

It is an invitation from God to choose between two ways of living out our faith.

One of these ways appears to be safer[2], better known, more predictable and less volatile, whilst the other way is full of unknowns, brimming over with inarticulable things that are yet to be seen.

God doesn't wish us to choose the right-hand fork for the sake of being a 'risk-taker', or for the sake of being 'radical'.

He is just giving us a choice.

This is not a choice between different practices, it is a choice within us, at the very centre of our hearts.

God is inviting each of us to experience life at a higher pace; a life not of predictable corners that are easy to navigate by our own efforts, but rather a life filled with twists and turns that prevent us from seeing too far ahead, and a flow so fast that too much paddling could actually unsettle our balance.

He isn't forcing us to choose one route over the other, but the option is there.

Sooner or later though, we will have to make our choice.

It seems odd to say that God will bless us either way, yet I firmly believe that He will, and indeed is.

---

2. We must remember that, ultimately, our safety is not dictated by our life choices or found in the paths we take. Safety is found within Christ. So whilst one path 'appears' to be safer, in the sense that it is easier to navigate and better known, both paths are actually as safe as each other, as both paths contain Jesus, our safeguard for all eternity.

Perhaps this is because He wants us to make our choice not from of stepping outside of His will, but from excitement at the t adventure He is laying out before us.

Perhaps this is a time of opportunity over obligation.

The Inner Door

It strikes me that some of us may have settled into a way of life that is not full.

It may be really good, but not quite full.

When we look at our lives in the mirror, at our passions and our decisions, what do we see?

God is living within our hearts in the form of His Spirit and is trying to get our attention from that dwelling place.

He is knocking on the inner door of our hearts, stirring us to look at ourselves once again, to re-evaluate what we have thought was long decided.

The passions and dreams that lie just beyond what we are willing to acknowledge even to ourselves, may well be God Himself stirring us and trying to get our attention.

Knocking on the inner door.

Seeking to have an audience with us.

Imploring us to make a choice to steer towards the rapids.

It's clear that God has not yet done all He wants to do by His Spirit on earth before His Son returns.

If He had, we wouldn't still be waiting!

As we *are* still waiting for Jesus' return, it must be the case that God has not yet finished pursuing all of His purposes on this earth.

What is more, we know that God adores working with His people, establishing His kingdom through our agreement with Him, so if He still has work to do before Jesus' return, we can be confident that it will involve you and me!

Because of His love of doing things with us, God has planted Himself inside of us.

Our redeemed hearts are designed to host part of God's plan for His world.

Within each of us is part of God's blueprint of restoration for the earth.

What if the things we have pushed aside, labelling them as 'youthful ignorance' and 'wishful thinking', are actually God at work within us forging a heavenly plan?

The disappointment of unfulfilled desires has led some of us to question whether having fire in our hearts is good and whether passionate feelings can ever be helpful.

We've called emotional drive 'immaturity', without truly contending to see the desires of our hearts redeemed and refined by God Himself.

Of course our hearts can mislead us; as we saw in *The Dying Fish*, the greater the truth given from God, the greater the twist that Satan can give it. But the fact that Satan *can* twist something does not mean we should fear it.

It would be crazy to abandon the truth just so the Devil can't twist it.

That's a bit like never using a kitchen knife because it is possible for it to cut you!

When something good and useful has the potential to be misused and harmful, we don't stop using it—we just use it with extra care.

God has set so much within our hearts and minds—He Himself lives there by His Spirit!

He made the effort to renew[3] them in order to write His voice within them.

The new covenant, as described in *Hebrews 8*, shows the high value God places on His people's hearts and minds. The new covenant is essentially an internal change, primarily designed to affect the core of who we are:

> *For this is the covenant that I will make with the house of*
> *Israel*
> *After those days, says the Lord:*
> *I will imprint My laws upon their minds, [even upon their*
> *innermost thoughts and*
> *understanding],*
> *and engrave them upon their hearts [effecting their*
> *regeneration].*
> *And I will be their God,*
> *And they shall be My people.*
> HEBREWS 8.10 AMP

Do you see?

Even though we could never have earned the right to invite God to make His home within our former selves, Christ has made us perfectly clean and sent His Spirit to take up residence in us.

---

3. *Romans 12.1* & *Ezekiel 36.26*.

The God who lives in you is leading you and speaking to you from within your very heart and mind.

He has written His precepts and principles within you!

Can you hear God knocking?

Can you hear Him stirring desire and passion?

What is He saying to you?

Open the inner door and begin to give the still small voice of God, present in your hopes and desires[4], audience and weight as you choose your next steps, and your path down the river.

Do Not Hide — *Part One*

Perhaps some of us have a sense of what God is saying through the inner door.

Perhaps it really excites us.

However, it is all too easy for our excitement about God's plan for us to revolve more around the outcome of those plans, than about God Himself.

We begin to be motivated by fruitfulness, success and influence.

But when we are truly whole, we are motivated by love.

It does not bother me that we have these moments when success tries to steal the motivation of our hearts.

---

4. God's voice is present elsewhere as well of course!

What saddens me is that we often hide from ourselves these moments, pretending that they aren't there.

Either we are ashamed of our hunger for success, and pretend if it does not exist, or we actually begin to see God as a spring for success.

We can reduce God to a means to an end.

We don't mean to, but that is what can start to happen.

Neither of those ways are true life, neither of those ways are what any of us are called to, and neither of those ways are what our hearts were made for.

We were made for the way of love, which is the way of Jesus Christ.[5]

Following the way of love means that success, according to this world, may come to us.

But it also may not.

If we want to put a mark on eternity, we must give up pursuing fruitfulness as our primary target.

Love's motivation is the object of its affection, not the outcome of its affection.

Jesus was motivated by His love for the Father, not by what fruit this love would have, and yet His life was exceptionally fruitful!

Instead of cloaking the funny little desires and motivations within us in the hope that no one will see them, let us bare our all before God, being honest with Him about our innermost parts.

---

5. *1 Corinthians 14.1.*

The Mirror

we are unwilling to admit to God the unspoken desires within us, then we are not giving Him permission to minister to us, to redeem our wants, or to use us in the perfect way that only He knows how.

We need to see ourselves clearly to understand our motivations and desires. If we do not see ourselves clearly then we can never be truly honest with God, because we cannot be honest with ourselves!

Turn your attention to yourself and ask the Spirit to show you what is really there.

Take a look.

Do Not Hide — *Part Two*

Others of us believe that we were made to be mundane.

Incapable of greatness, success or influence.

We don't struggle with idolising success or greatness because we cannot believe that success or greatness are possibilities for us.

But the truth of the matter is that God has designed us all to be significant; He has designed us all for greatness.

Significant not necessarily in the eyes of the world, but certainly in the eyes of God.

If we have placed our faith in Jesus, God has changed our nature into the nature of Jesus by His grace and power.[6]

And the nature of Jesus is great.[7]

---

6. *2 Peter 1.4.*

7. I use the word '*great*' here to mean astounding, remarkable, *(cont. on next page)*

Very great indeed.

If we now have *His* nature, then it must be true that we are great, because Jesus could not be any greater!

Not for our own benefit, not by our own doing, and certainly not by our own wisdom.

All by God's grace and for His delight.

We have a choice, either to believe that God desires to work in, with and through us, or not.

How gracious is God! He has achieved everything needed to make us whole and free, yet places the decision back into our hands as to whether we accept His invitation of limitless transformation.

If we put limits on what He is capable of doing in our lives, we misunderstand the nature of our re-birth by the Holy Spirit.

He makes all things possible.

That's simply who He is and what He does.

In other words, the Holy Spirit's work in us knows no boundaries.

Let's wake up.

God has been incredibly good to us and His goodness will continue to unfold today and for all eternity.

We owe Him everything.

Our lives no longer belong to us.

---

wonderful, incredible, significant... so the list could go on!

Our lives now belong to Him.

We do not have the luxury of saying that we cannot be something; God makes us able for anything to which He calls us.

Can you hear Him knocking? Is He stirring you?

It is time to shake disbelief and a low self-esteem from your shoulders and replace it with the opinion of Jesus Christ.

That's true humility.

He is not angry with you, but He is furious at the accusing voices, the debilitating lies and the ensnaring insecurities that are trying to steal you away from Him, and steal you away from who He made you to be!

He wants to throw all your insecurities further away from you than you can possibly imagine.

All of your shakiness and uncertainty need not lead you to hide from Jesus.

He isn't put off by wobbly knees.[8]

What Are You For?

It is so easy for our lives to become centred upon obtaining and holding onto certain things.

Whether it be a stable career, a functional, loving family, enduring friendships or even simply having fun, so many things can threaten to become the centre of our day-to-day existence.

---

8. *Psalm 147.10-11.*

But why would we spend our lives striving to grasp something that God loves to give to us freely?[9]

When Jesus told His disciples to:

> *Seek first the kingdom of God and his righteousness, and all these things will be added to you.*
> MATTHEW 6.33 ESV

He really meant what He said.

God wants to give us good gifts because He is good. He wants to give us these gifts freely, not as a result of our effort. We can therefore leave all things to Him and throw all of our effort into what He is asking of us.

To delight in seeking Him and His kingdom.

Our responsibility is to whole-heartedly seek Him and He is responsible for everything else.

Through seeking Him, He will unravel specific kingdom causes[10] that He would like us to give ourselves to.

I do not know what God is specifically asking you to give yourself to, and you may not either, but that is okay.

It's only through pro-actively giving God an all-access invitation to our lives that we will begin to see what He desires us to give ourselves to.

---

9. Of course, God may not give every person who lives for Him everything listed above. They are examples of some of the blessings God loves to give, however, we will each be given different gifts from God. If God withholds certain gifts from us it is not because we are less favorable to Him or less loved, it is in His wisdom and perfection that He chooses what to give. And whilst He invites us to continually ask Him for things in prayer, we must be content with what He gives, rather than focusing on what He doesn't.

10. I've borrowed the phrase *"kingdom cause"* from my good friend Tim.

But we will not give Him that invitation unless we truly love Him.

And as we know, we will not love Him unless we continually encounter His love for us; and we cannot encounter His love for us without encountering Him.

Do you see that your pursuit of God is where the unfolding of your life truly begins?

No one can teach you how you are to pursue Him.

My dearest friend Nathaniel pursues God differently to me.

Nathaniel has not been taught how he should love Jesus. In fact, when people tried to tell him how he should pursue Jesus, it put him off a bit.

I have absolutely no doubt that Nathaniel loves Jesus incredibly deeply, but he expresses it in his way.

He doesn't think arrogantly about his way of loving God, he just does it. It is him being him, with God.

Simple.

How about you?

Do you know how *you* love God? Or are you just imitating what you've seen of other people's pursuit of God?

Of course, as I have said before, God often speaks to us through others.

God will use others to inspire us in our personal walk with Him and He will ask others to challenge us and to encourage us. We must notbecome isolated and hard hearted to the input of others under the guise of 'protecting our walk with Jesus'; that is unscriptural.[11]

However, it is important that we each build a deeply personal and individual friendship with God in the midst of our fellowship with others.

God is inviting us each to forge our own, unique relationship with Him that cannot be shaken or stolen by any scheme of hell or of humankind.

And from this pursuit of God, we will see the things of God flow from His throne into our lives.

So let us not settle for giving ourselves to any other thing than the pursuit of God.

Let us trust that all we need, and even every godly want within us, will be given to us as a free gift, thanks to the benevolence of our kindly Father in heaven, as we give ourselves to seeking Him with all that we have within us.

The Eternal Vision

Whilst our pursuit of Christ is unique to each of us, we are also a part of God's global church, following Jesus together.

Each of us has been given different gifts from God. We are all different people, designed to be different parts of the body of Christ.[12] But when we bring those gifts together, we enable the body to function.

We are one body made up of many parts.

---

11. *Proverbs 27.17 & Hebrews 10.24-25.*

12. *1 Corinthians 12.12-31.*

This reality is designed to seep into our attitudes and practices as well. It's not right to say that we're part of the body, yet live lives disconnected from others.

The best way to connect with others is to find common vision.

For vision binds people together, it holds them fast:

> *Where there is no vision [no revelation of God and His word],*
> *the people are unrestrained;*
> *But happy and blessed is he who keeps the law [of God].*
> PROVERBS 29.18 AMP

Knowing what a powerful, constructive thing vision can be, we often spend a lot of time searching for it.

Whether it be for our lives, our marriages, our work, our churches or even just for today.

But *Proverbs 29.18* doesn't suggest that finding a vision is the solution for a visionless, unrestrained people.

Proverbs 29.18 tells us that keeping God's law is the remedy for a lack of vision.

And we know that Jesus fulfilled the entire law of the old covenant.[13]

He is the law's fulfilment!

According to *Proverbs 29.18*, keeping God's law is the only way to have true vision, and the only person who can, and has, fulfilled God's law, is Jesus.

This means that the only solution to not having vision is to follow

---

13. *Matthew 5.17.*

Jesus, for He is the only one who has been able to keep God's law.

He is the one vision that is truly eternal.

The one vision that will satisfy and nurture us forever.

The person of Jesus Christ.

At the end of the day, the vision that will bind redeemed humankind together for all eternity is God Himself.

Why not just have following Him as our vision?

Yes, having Jesus Christ as our vision will look different for each of us, and God gives His people different sections of His kingdom to establish on earth at different times; but underneath the personal and individual differences, what is the one element that connects them all?

What is the the one, united vision?

Christianity is based around a real person who is active amongst us today. He is powerful, and He is relentless.

He doesn't always say comfortable things, or act as we would advise Him to.

But He *is* God.

And He *is* good.

As you put this book down, perhaps sit back in your chair and reflect for just a moment.

Are you really passionate about Jesus?

Not a measured passion that we can communicate in tidy phrases, but one that can only be described as a response to the surpassing glory of God Himself.

Are you *actually* following Him?

'Following Him' does not just mean that you have faith in Him, but that you are responding to His call daily, delighting in seeking Him and enjoying your friendship with Him.

Are you being faithful with what He has revealed to you?

Do you love Him?

Not just with the calculated, mental love of choice, but also with a hearty, emotional, all-in love?

Stop and ask yourself;

"Is my vision, at its core, truly and simply just Him?"

Christ alone.

The Gospel.

The Good News That Keeps Getting Better.

EPILOGUE

Do Not Go Beyond Simplicity

My hope is that in reading this book you will have been inspired by Jesus Christ Himself, by His love, goodness and kindness.

I hope that you have seen more of Him.

Perhaps you will have heard Him whisper the life-changing, life-bringing words afresh;

"Follow me."

For at its heart, Christianity is about continually responding to that invitation.

It is all too easy to create a complex version of Christianity that, ironically, takes us away from the simplicity of the Gospel; the simplicity of responding to the *"follow me"* of Jesus Christ.

In order to respond whole-heartedly to His invitation to follow Him, we must have great integrity.

I am aware that in some of my writing I talk about a way of faith in Jesus that could be abused; that people could perhaps misuse some of what I have said to give themselves license to pursue ungodly things.

But as I thought about how to present what I believe to be true, I could not find a way around this.

It has led me to the conclusion that Jesus left Himself open to be abused, both in what He taught, and in how He lived.

When He taught His disciples to turn the other cheek[1], 77 times[2], He was showing them how His way of life leav live by it open to ill-treatment.

We forgive, yet those who persecute may not.

So Jesus tells us to forgive again.

And again.

Forgiveness, love, kindness, purity and many other aspects of Jesus' character that His Spirit wants to form within us, begin in the heart and work their way out to our actions.

Jesus' teaching on the significance of the heart was, and still is, revolutionary because it leaves us no room to judge others by a set of 'correct' or 'incorrect' rules.

Instead, it encourages us to confront the state of our own hearts.

Doesn't Jesus repeatedly bring this very issue to our attention in the gospels? Doesn't He continually point out those who *look* like they are doing the right thing but whose hearts tell another story?

Does He not draw special attention to those who are ignored by the majority, deemed unworthy, impure and unclean, yet who are seen and praised by God because of their internal faith, godliness and love?

This is why truly following Jesus demands and requires total integrity.

Throughout history some people have twisted Scripture in order to legitimise doing terrible things.

---

1. *Matthew 5.38-40.*

2. *Mathew 18.22.*

Jesus' words have been used to justify condemnation, judgement, anger, revenge, murder and many other atrocities that He specifically spoke against.

But it is of the highest importance that we do not abandon teaching the truth of Scripture for fear that some may abuse it.

We must not dilute Scripture, under-emphasise the more challenging parts, or try to over-explain the mysterious God we follow in an attempt to stop people abusing it.

The solution is not to adapt the truth in an attempt to prevent it being twisted.

I believe the answer is to preach and live truth plainly and simply so that distortions will be seen for what they are.

We must cling to the truth all the more strongly.

At the end of the day, the most important thing each of us can do is to personally pursue the person of Jesus, continually bringing our whole hearts before Him, not to justify any ungodly wants, but to be refined by His love.

From the biggest decision to follow Him, to the smallest decisions of each day, if we want to walk in the richness of life that following Jesus offers, we must choose to bring every inch of ourselves into our relationship with Him.

We are responsible for ourselves, and when Jesus returns He will ask about us. He won't ask us for our opinion on how those around us have done, or whether we thought person 'x' treated person 'y' correctly.

He is interested in each of us.

He will talk with you about your thoughts, beliefs, fears, judgements, anger and insecurities.

You'll be talking about the inside state of you.

But His interest and passion about your mind and heart will not suddenly start when He returns; it is what He is passionate about now.

It's what He's always been passionate about.

So be honest with yourself.

Take off all pretence and don't hide any longer.

Right now Jesus is speaking to you; both eyes focussed on you, and His voice addressing just you;

"Follow me."

The simplest of invitations from one so full of complexities and intricacies.

The complex simplicity of following Jesus.

"Follow me."

Will you?

Made in the USA
Columbia, SC
26 February 2018